THE THEOLOGY OF THE CHURCH:

A BIBLIOGRAPHY

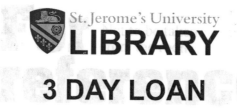

THE THEOLOGY OF THE CHURCH:

A BIBLIOGRAPHY

Avery Dulles, S.J.
&
Patrick Granfield, O.S.B.

PAULIST PRESS
New York/Mahwah, N.J.

Book design by Theresa M. Sparacio

Cover design by Moe Berman

Library of Congress Cataloging-in-Publication Data

Dulles, Avery Robert,   1918–
    The theology of the church : a bibliography / Avery Dulles &
Patrick Granfield.
       p.   cm.
    Includes index.
    ISBN 0–8091–3847–6 (alk. paper)
    1. Church—Bibliography. 2. Catholic Church—Doctrines—Bibliography.
I. Granfield, Patrick. II. Title.
Z7776.7.D84   1999
[BX1746]
016.262–dc21   98–45037
                                                                          CIP

Published by Paulist Press
997 Macarthur Boulevard
Mahwah, New Jersey 07430

www.paulistpress.com   MAY 0 1 2000

Printed and bound in the
United States of America

CONTENTS

Introduction 1

1. Bibliographies 5

2. Survey Articles 7

3. Collected Readings 9

4. Festschriften 10

5. Official Roman Catholic Documents 14

6. Classics of Ecclesiology 17

7. History of Ecclesiology 19

8. New Testament 20

9. The Patristic Era 25

10. St. Augustine 27

11. The Middle Ages 29

12. St. Thomas Aquinas 32

13. The Reformation 34

14. The Seventeenth through the Nineteenth Centuries 36

15. Vatican Council I 38

16. Vatican Council II 41

17. Trends in Twentieth-Century Roman
    Catholic Ecclesiology. 46

18. Twentieth-Century Orthodox Ecclesiology. 51

19. Twentieth-Century Protestant and
    Anglican Ecclesiology 55

20. The Nature of the Church 59

21. The Church as Body of Christ and People of God. 64

22. The Church as One, Holy, Catholic, and Apostolic 66

23. The Holiness of the Church 69

24. The Unity of the Church. 71

25. Membership in the Church. 79

26. The Church and Salvation:
    The Necessity of the Church 81

27. Evangelization and Missionary Activity. 83

28. The Church and Sacramentality 88

29. The Church as Communion. 91

30. Basic Ecclesial Communities 94

31. The Church as Institution and Structure 97

32. Continuity, Structural Change, and Reform. 100

33. The Sociology of the Church 102

34. Freedom and Participation in the Church 105

35. The Papacy. 107

36. Episcopacy and Collegiality 113

37. The Teaching Office 118

38. Infallibility 123

39. Councils: Ecumenical, National, and Diocesan 126

40. The Synod of Bishops and the Episcopal Conference. . . 129

41. The Particular or Local Church 132

42. The Parish 136

43. Charisms in the Church 140

44. Ordained Ministers in the Church: 143
        A. The Priesthood. 143
        B. The Diaconate. 147

45. Religious in the Church 149

46. Laity in the Church 152

47. Women in the Church. 157

48. The "Sense of the Faithful". 160

49. The Church in the World:
    The Social Mission of the Church 162

50. Liberation Ecclesiology. 165

51. The Multicultural Church: 170
        A. General Studies 170
        B. Hispanic/Latino Ecclesiology. 171
        C. African and African-American Ecclesiology 172
        D. Asian Ecclesiology 173
        E. Native American Ecclesiology. 175

52. Mary and the Church 176

53. The Church, the Kingdom, and the Eschaton 179

Index of Names. 181

Please Note

*An asterisk before a title indicates that the work
is of broad interest and serves as
a good introduction to the topic.*

INTRODUCTION

Ecclesiology is the theological discipline that systematically studies the nature, mission, and structure of the church of Jesus Christ. As an organized body of knowledge, however, ecclesiology appeared relatively late in the history of Christian theology. Neither the writers of the New Testament nor the Fathers wrote formal treatises on the church. Yet both gave us an abundance of profound ecclesial reflections. For them the communion of believers in Christ is an essential part of the self-revelation of God, and its mission is to proclaim sanctification and salvation.

St. Thomas Aquinas did not write a separate theology of the church in his *Summa Theologiae,* but he discussed the church in his treatment of the Mystical Body of Christ and the sacraments. In the late Middle Ages theologians often wrote to defend the rights of the papacy and to clarify the relationship between the spiritual and the secular power.

The first treatise of ecclesiology is generally attributed to James of Viterbo, an Augustinian priest who was a professor at Paris and later archbishop of Naples. He wrote *De regimine christiano* in 1301–1302. Later, during the Reformation and the Counter Reformation, there were many texts on ecclesiology, but none more comprehensive and incisive than the multivolume *De controversiis* of Robert Bellarmine, which influenced the development of ecclesiology for centuries. From the sixteenth century to the middle of the twentieth, most of the ecclesiological works had a controversial and juridical tone.

Significant changes, however, occurred in the course of the

1

twentieth century, which Otto Dibelius, a Lutheran theologian, called the "century of the church." Relying on the results of significant scriptural, patristic, liturgical, and historical research, theologians began to develop a richer and more balanced ecclesiology. They realized that a sound theology of the church is essential in order to understand the varied ways God works in the world through Christ and his Spirit.

The Second Vatican Council (1962–1965) concentrated on the church and in so doing revitalized ecclesiology. The council treated the church in a sacramental, pastoral, and ecumenical perspective and elaborated the relationship between the church on earth and the final kingdom of God. By recognizing the church as mystery and communion, the council situated the respective roles of the hierarchy, clergy, religious, and laity in a communitarian context. Vatican II, committed to the healing of the division among Christians, stressed the common bonds and vital links between Roman Catholic, Orthodox, and Protestant Christians. It also viewed positively those salvific elements found in non-Christian religions.

A vast amount of published material has appeared since the council. As a result, it has become increasingly difficult to keep abreast of the many books, monographs, and articles dealing with ecclesiological topics. Teachers and students have their own "To Be Read" list that, unfortunately, grows faster than they can read it all. At times, they may feel overwhelmed in trying to keep abreast of the current works in ecclesiology. In the quest to be current, it is easy to neglect those solid works of earlier generations.

The purpose of this bibliography is to present some of the most important ecclesiological writings, both past and present. Our selection of work goes through the year 1998. Although the listing is extensive, it does not claim to be exhaustive. Since a bibliography that is too long and undifferentiated may be of little help, we have divided the material into several categories, each with a limited number of items. Works of general interest that may help to introduce the theme are indicated by an asterisk.

An ecclesial dimension touches every aspect of theology, but we have restricted our focus to the nature, mission, and structure of the church in order to make our task manageable. Titles have been selected for their historical value, reliability, and utility. English translations of foreign works are given when available. Due to limited space, we have, for the most part, listed books rather than articles. Yet many of the books cited have bibliographies that contain extensive references to the periodical literature.

Certain topics have been omitted, not because they are totally unrelated to ecclesiology but because they deserve their own specialized bibliographies. In this category would fall such subjects as sacraments, liturgy, catechetics, interreligious dialogue, canon law, and the struggle between the church and civil society. Although we have separate sections on ecumenism and missiology, both of those topics are too broad to be fully treated here.

The literature on ecclesiology has grown considerably since we published the now out-of-print book *The Church: A Bibliography* (Wilmington, Del.: Michael Glazier, 1985). In the present volume, we have added over six hundred new items, deleted some of the earlier references, and created two new categories dealing with the Multicultural Church and Mary and the Church. New items are found in every one of the sections. This new material graphically illustrates what are some of the major contemporary interests in ecclesiology. Thus, the following categories have the most new references: Vatican Council II, Trends in Twentieth-Century Roman Catholic Ecclesiology, Twentieth-Century Orthodox Ecclesiology, The Unity of the Church, The Church as Communion, The Papacy, Ordained Ministers in the Church, and The Laity in the Church.

The intended readers of this bibliography are those interested in the theology of the church. We prepared this book principally with Roman Catholic readers in mind; but it can be used profitably by others as well, since it includes much material of interest to the wider Christian world. Professional theologians, students, Christian educators, clergy, and concerned laity may approach this book differently, but all will find something helpful for their own special needs.

Many people have generously contributed suggestions to this book. We are particularly grateful for those offered by Gerard Austin, O.P., Patrick Cogan, S.A., Robert B. Eno, S.S., John T. Ford, C.S.C., Robert Fox, John P. Galvin, Christopher O'Donnell,

O.Carm., and Peter C. Phan. Special thanks are due to two people for their outstanding assistance: R. Bruce Miller of the Religious Studies/Humanities Division of Mullen Library at The Catholic University of America, who helped us in innumerable ways; and James Kruggel, a doctoral student at Catholic University, for his research skills and computer expertise.

Finally, we hope that this bibliography on the theology of the church will prove to be a valuable tool for those who are desirous of learning more about the mystery of the community of disciples. The following prayer of St. Paul reminds us that, as we try to understand the various facets of the mystery of the church of Christ, we should not lose sight of the ultimate reason for our efforts:

> Out of his infinite glory, may he give you the power through his Spirit for your hidden life to grow strong, so that Christ may live in your hearts through faith, and then, planted in love and built on love, you will with all the saints have strength to grasp the breadth and the length, the height and the depth; until, knowing the love of Christ, which is beyond all knowledge, you are filled with the utter fullness of God (Ephesians 3:16–19).

Avery Dulles, S.J.　　　　　*Patrick Granfield, O.S.B.*
Fordham University　　　　The Catholic University of America

BIBLIOGRAPHIES

Blockx, Karel. *Bibliographical Introduction to Church History*. Leuven: Acco, 1982.

"Bulletin d'ecclésiologie." In *Revue des sciences philosophiques et théologiques*. For many years it was written by Yves Congar. His last contribution was in 1988.

Congar, Yves M.-J. "Chroniques." In *Sainte Église*, 448–696. Unam Sanctam, no. 41. Paris: Cerf, 1963.

Dupuy, Bernard-Dominique. "Le mystère de l'Église: Bibliographie organisée." *La vie spirituelle* 104 (1961): 70–85.

Ephemerides theologicae lovanienses. Annual "Elenchus bibliographicus."

Ford, David F., ed. *The Modern Theologians: An Introduction to Christian Theology in the Twentieth Century*. 2nd ed. New York/Oxford: Blackwell, 1989.

Jossua, Jean-Pierre, and Yves M.-J. Congar. *Theology in the Service of God's People*. Chicago: Priory, 1968. Bibliography of Congar through 1967.

Musser, Donald W., and Joseph L. Price, eds. *A New Handbook of Christian Theologians*. Nashville, Tenn.: Abingdon, 1996.

Nichols, Aidan. "An Yves Congar Bibliography 1967–1987." *Angelicum* 66 (1989): 422–66.

Valeske, Ulrich. *Votum Ecclesiae.* Pt. 2, pp. 1–210. Munich: Claudius, 1962.

ATLA (American Theological Library Association) publishes several semiannual, annual, and retrospective indexes to religious literature that contain extensive listings and book review citations. See especially *Religion Index One: Periodicals; Religion Index Two: Multi-Author Works and Festschriften;* and *Research in Ministry*—an index of D.Min. projects and theses submitted by members of the Association of Theological Schools.

CERDIC (Centre de recherches et de documentation des institutions chrétiennes) of the University of Strasbourg publishes several computerized bibliographies. The following are valuable for ecclesiology: *RIC* (Répertoire bibliographique des institutions chrétiennes) and its *Suppléments: Oecuménisme; Hommes et Église; Recherches institutionnelles;* and *État et religion.*

Other useful sources for bibliographical information are the following: *Bulletin de théologie ancienne et médiévale; Bulletin signalétique* (n.527—*Sciences religieuses*); *Catholic Periodical and Literature Index* (English language); *Internationale oekumenische Bibliographie; Theologische Literaturzeitung;* and *Theologische Revue.*

SURVEY ARTICLES

Granfield, Patrick. "Ecclesiology." In *New Catholic Encyclopedia*, vol. 18, Supplement: 1978–1988, 128–31. Washington, D.C.: Jack Heraty & Associates with Catholic University of America, 1989.

Kress, Robert. "Church (Theology)." In *New Catholic Encyclopedia*, vol. 17, Supplement: Change in the Church, 1979, 116–21. Washington, D.C. and New York: Publishers Guild with McGraw-Hill, 1979.

Lawlor, Francis X. "Church. II. (Theology of)." In *New Catholic Encyclopedia*, 3:683–93. New York: McGraw-Hill, 1967.

Le Guillou, Marie-Joseph, Karl Rahner, and Emilio Sauras. "Church." In *Sacramentum Mundi*, 1:313–37. New York: Herder and Herder, 1968. Articles of Le Guillou and Rahner reprinted in *Encyclopedia of Theology: The Concise Sacramentum Mundi*, 205–27. New York: Seabury, 1975.

Lerch, Joseph R. "Ecclesiology." In *New Catholic Encyclopedia*, 5:34–35. New York: McGraw-Hill, 1967.

O'Donnell, Christopher. *Ecclesia: A Theological Encyclopedia of the Church*. Collegeville, Minn.: Liturgical Press, 1996. Each entry has an extensive bibliography.

The following sources contain much helpful historical and theological information on the Church: *Bibellexikon; Catholicisme; Dictionary of Fundamental Theology; Dictionnaire d'archéologie et de liturgie; Dictionnaire de droit canonique; Dictionnaire de la Bible, Supplément; Dictionnaire d'histoire et de géographie ecclésiastiques; Dictionnaire de théologie; Dictionnaire de théologie catholique; Dizionario teologico interdisciplinare; Encyclopedia of American Church History; Enciclopedia cattolica; Enciclopedia de la religión católica, Encyclopaedia Britannica; Encyclopedic Dictionary of Religion; Evangelisches Kirchenlexikon; Handbook of Catholic Theology; HarperCollins Encyclopedia of Catholicism; Lexikon für Theologie und Kirche; Modern Catholic Encyclopedia; New Dictionary of Theology; Our Sunday Visitor's Catholic Encyclopedia; Oxford Dictionary of the Christian Church; Realenzyklopädie für protestantische Theologie; Reallexikon für Antike und Christentum; Die Religion in Geschichte und Gegenwart* (selections from the 2nd ed.: Jaroslav Pelikan, ed. *Twentieth-Century Theology in the Making.* 3 vols. New York: Harper & Row; London: Fontana, 1969–70); and *Theologische Realenzyklopädie.*

3

COLLECTED READINGS

Burns, Patrick J., ed. *Mission and Witness.* Westminster, Md.: Newman, 1965.

Dirkswager, Edward J., Jr., ed. *Readings in the Theology of the Church.* Englewood Cliffs, N.J.: Prentice-Hall, 1970.

Rahner, Hugo, et al. *The Church: Readings in Theology.* Compiled at the Canisianum, Innsbruck. New York: Kenedy, 1963.

4

FESTSCHRIFTEN

Anderson, H. George, and James R. Crumley, eds. *Promoting Unity: Themes in Lutheran–Catholic Dialogue.* Minneapolis: Augsburg Fortress, 1989. Festschrift for Johannes Cardinal Willebrands.

Auer, Johann, and Hermann Volk, eds. *Theologie in Geschichte und Gegenwart: Michael Schmaus zum sechzigsten Geburtstag.* Munich: K. Zink, 1957.

Baier, Walter, et al., eds. *Weisheit Gottes–Weisheit der Welt: Festschrift für Joseph Kardinal Ratzinger.* St. Ottilien: EOS, 1987.

Bäumer, Remigius, and Heimo Dolch, eds. *Volk Gottes: Festgabe für J. Höfer.* Freiburg: Herder, 1967.

Beales, Derek, and Geoffrey Best, eds. *History, Society, and the Churches: Essays in Honor of Owen Chadwick.* New York: Cambridge University, 1985.

Bockmuehl, Markus, and Michael B. Thompson, eds. *A Vision for the Church: Studies in Early Christian Ecclesiology in Honour of J. P. M. Sweet.* Edinburgh: T & T Clark, 1997.

Carmody, Denise Lardner, and John Tully Carmody, eds. *The Future of Prophetic Christianity: Essays in Honor of Robert McAfee Brown.* Maryknoll, N.Y.: Orbis, 1993.

Chica, F., S. Panizzolo, and H. Wagner, eds. *Ecclesia Tertii Millennii*

Advenientis: Omaggio al P. Angel Antón. Casale Monferrato: Piemme, 1997.

Daniélou, Jean, and Herbert Vorgrimler, eds. *Sentire Ecclesiam: Festgabe H. Rahner.* Freiburg: Herder, 1961. Historical Studies.

Editorial Committee of the *Ephemerides theologicae lovanienses. Ecclesia a Spiritu Sancto edocta: Mélanges théologiques à Mgr. Gérard Philips.* Gembloux: J. Duculot, 1970.

Efroymson, David, and John Raines, eds. *Open Catholicism: The Tradition at Its Best. Essays in Honor of Gerard S. Sloyan.* Collegeville, Minn.: Liturgical Press, 1977.

Ellis, Mark H., and Otto Maduro, eds. *The Future of Liberation Theology: Essays in Honor of Gustavo Gutiérrez.* Maryknoll, N.Y.: Orbis, 1989.

Evans, Gillian R., ed. *Christian Authority: Essays in Honour of Henry Chadwick.* New York: Oxford University Press and Oxford: Clarendon, 1988.

Evans, Gillian R., and Michel Gourgues, eds. *Communion et Réunion: Mélanges Jean-Marie Roger Tillard.* Leuven: Leuven University Press and Uitgeverij Peeters, 1995.

Fraling, Bernhard, Helmut Hoping, and Juan Carlos Scannone, eds. *Kirche und Theologie im kulturellen Dialog: Für Peter Hünermann.* Freiburg: Herder, 1994.

Gassmann, Günther, and Peder Nørgaard-Højen, eds. *Einheit der Kirche: Neue Entwicklungen und Perspektiven. Harding Meyer zum 60. Geburtstag.* Frankfurt am Main: Lembeck, 1988.

Geerlings, Wilhelm, and Max Seckler, eds. *Kirche sein: Nachkonziliare Theologie in Dienst der Kirchenreform. Für Hermann Josef Pottmeyer.* Freiburg: Herder, 1994.

Geffré, Claude, N. B. Rettenbach, and D. J. Robert, eds. *L'hommage différé au Père Chenu.* Paris: Cerf, 1990.

Granfield, Patrick, and Josef A. Jungmann, eds. *Kyriakon:*

Festschrift Johannes Quasten. 2 vols. Münster: Aschendorff, 1970.

Hagen, Kenneth, ed., *The Quadrilog: Tradition and the Future of Ecumenism. Essays in Honor of George H. Tavard.* Collegeville, Minn.: Liturgical Press, 1994.

Hein, Lorenz, ed. *Die Einheit der Kirche: Dimensionen ihrer Heiligkeit, Katholizität, und Apostolizität. Festgabe Peter Meinhold zum 70. Geburtstag.* Wiesbaden: Steiner, 1977.

Hills, Julian V., ed. *Common Life in the Early Church. Essays Honoring Graydon F. Snyder.* Harrisburg, Penn.: Trinity Press International, 1998.

Hultgren, Arland J., and Barbara Hall, eds. *Christ and His Communities: Essays in Honor of Reginald H. Fuller. Anglican Theological Review.* Supplement No. 11 (March 1990) 1–153.

The Jurist 56/1 (1996). This entire issue is a Festschrift for Ladislas Örsy.

Klinger, Elmar, and Klaus Wittstadt, eds. *Glaube im Prozess: Christsein nach dem II. Vatikanum. Für Karl Rahner.* Freiburg: Herder, 1984.

Lamb, Matthew, ed. *Creativity and Method: Essays in Honor of Bernard Lonergan.* Milwaukee, Wis.: Marquette University, 1991.

Lorcin, Marie-Thérèse, et al., eds. *Papauté, monachisme, et théories politiques: Études d'histoire mediévale offertes à Marcel Pacaut. 1, Le pouvoir et l'institution ecclésiale; 2, Les églises locales.* Lyon: Presses Universitaires de Lyon, 1994.

Lutz-Bachmann, Matthias, ed. *Und dennoch ist von Gott zu reden: Festschrift für Herbert Vorgrimler.* Freiburg: Herder, 1994.

Mackie, Robert, and Charles West, eds. *The Sufficiency of God: Essays on the Ecumenical Hope in Honor of W. A. Visser't Hooft.* London: SCM, 1963.

Melloni, Alberto, Daniele Menozzi, Giuseppe Ruggieri, and Massimo Toschi, eds. *Cristianesimo nella Storia: Saggi in onore di Giuseppe Alberigo.* Bologna: Il Mulino, 1996.

Nassif, Bradley, ed. *New Perspectives on Historical Theology: Essays in Memory of John Meyendorff.* Grand Rapids, Mich., and Cambridge, U.K.: Wm. B. Eerdmans, 1996.

Neiman, David, and Margaret Schatkin, eds. *The Heritage of the Early Church: Essays in Honor of Georges Vasilievich Florovsky.* Rome: Institute of Oriental Studies, 1973.

Neuner, Peter, and Harald Wagner, *In Verantwortung für den Glauben: Beiträge zur Fundamentaltheologie und Ökumenik für Heinrich Fries.* Freiburg: Herder, 1992.

O'Donovan, Leo J., and T. Howland Sanks, eds. *Faithful Witness: Foundations of Theology for Today's Church.* New York: Crossroad, 1989. This volume is in honor of Avery Dulles.

Phan, Peter C., ed. *Church and Theology: Essays in Memory of Carl J. Peter.* Washington, D.C.: Catholic University of America, 1995.

Pinto de Oliveira, Carlos-Josephat, ed. *Ordo Sapientiae et Amoris: Hommage au Professeur Jean-Pierre Torrell, O.P.* Fribourg: Editions Universitaires, 1993.

Reding, Marcel, ed. *Abhandlungen über Theologie und Kirche: Festschrift für Karl Adam.* Düsseldorf: Patmos, 1952.

Schockenhoff, Eberhard, and Peter Walter, eds. *Dogma und Glaube: Bausteine für eine theologische Erkenntnislehre: Festschrift für Bischof Walter Kasper.* Mainz: Matthias-Grünewald, 1993.

Schwaiger, Georg, ed. *Konzil und Papst: Historische Beiträge zur Frage der höchsten Gewalt in der Kirche. Festschrift für Hermann Tüchle.* Paderborn: F. Schöningh, 1968.

Weitlauff, Manfred, and Karl Hausberger, eds. *Papsttum und Kirchenreform: Historische Beiträge. Festschrift für Georg Schwaiger.* St. Ottilien: EOS, 1990.

5

OFFICIAL ROMAN CATHOLIC DOCUMENTS

Catechism of the Catholic Church. Vatican City: Libreria Editrice Vaticana, 1994. §§ 748–975. Section on the church.

Congregation for the Doctrine of the Faith. *Mysterium ecclesiae. Acta Apostolicae Sedis* 65 (1973): 396–408. English translation: "Declaration in Defense of the Catholic Doctrine on the Church against Certain Errors of the Present." *Catholic Mind* 71 (1973): 54–64.

Enchiridion Vaticanum: Documenti ufficiali del concilio Vaticano II e della Santa Sede. Bologna: Dehoniane, 1962–.

Gremillion, Joseph, ed. *The Gospel of Peace and Justice: Catholic Social Teaching since Pope John*. Maryknoll, N.Y.: Orbis, 1976.

John Paul II. *Redemptor Hominis. Acta Apostolicae Sedis* 71 (1979): 257–324. English translation: *The Papal Encyclicals 1958–1981*, edited by Claudia Carlen, 245–73. Wilmington, N.C.: McGrath, 1981.

Leo XIII. *Satis cognitum. Acta Sanctae Sedis* 28 (1895–96): 708–39. English translation: *The Papal Encyclicals 1878–1903*, edited by Claudia Carlen, 387–404. Wilmington, N.C.: McGrath, 1981.

O'Brien, David J., and Thomas A. Shannon, eds. *Renewing the Earth: Catholic Documents on Peace, Justice and Liberation.* Garden City, N.Y.: Doubleday Image, 1977.

Papal Teachings: The Church. Selected and arranged by the Benedictine Monks of Solesmes. Boston: St. Paul, 1962.

Paul VI. *Ecclesiam suam. Acta Apostolicae Sedis* 56 (1964): 609–59. English translation: *The Papal Encyclicals 1958–1981,* edited by Claudia Carlen, 135–60. Wilmington, N.C.: McGrath, 1981.

————. *Evangelii nuntiandi. Acta Apostolicae Sedis* 68 (1976): 5–76. English translation: *Evangelization in the Modern World.* Washington, D.C.: USCC, 1976.

Pius XII. *Mystici corporis. Acta Apostolicae Sedis* 35 (1943): 193–248. English translation: *The Papal Encyclicals 1939–1958,* edited by Claudia Carlen, 35–63. Wilmington, N.C.: McGrath, 1981.

Synod of Bishops (1971). *The Ministerial Priesthood and Justice in the World.* Washington, D.C.: NCCB, 1971.

Synod of Bishops (1985). *A Message to the People of God and the Final Report. Origins* (Dec. 19, 1985): 441, 443–50.

Vatican Council I. *Supremi pastoris (Prima schema constitutionis de ecclesia Christi).* Latin text in *Sacrorum conciliorum nova et amplissima collectio,* edited by J. D. Mansi, 51:539–53. Florence, 1759ff.; Paris and Leipzig, 1901–27. Partial English translation in *The Church Teaches,* edited by J. E. Clarkson et al., 87–94. St. Louis, Mo.: B. Herder, 1955.

————. *Tametsi Deus (Schema constitutionis dogmaticae secundae de ecclesia Christi).* Prepared by Joseph Kleutgen. Latin text and the *Relatio* by Kleutgen in *Sacrorum conciliorum nova et amplissima collectio,* edited by J. D. Mansi, 53:308–32. Florence, 1759ff.; Paris and Leipzig, 1901–27.

————. *Pastor aeternus (Constitutio dogmatica de ecclesia Christi)*. Latin text in *Sacrorum conciliorum nova et amplissima collectio*, edited by J. D. Mansi, 52:1330–34. Florence, 1759ff.; Paris and Leipzig, 1901–27. English translation with Latin text in *Dublin Review* 67 (1870): 496–507.

Vatican Council II. *Acta et documenta concilio oecumenico Vaticano II apparando. Series I (Antepraeparatoria)*. Vatican City: Typis Polyglottis Vaticanis, 1960–61.

————. *Acta et documenta concilio oecumenico Vaticano II apparando. Series II (Praeparatoria)*. Vatican City: Typis Polyglottis Vaticanis, 1964–69.

————. *Acta synodalia sacrosancti concilii oecumenici Vaticani II*. Vatican City: Typis Polyglottis Vaticanis, 1970–80.

————. *Ad gentes. Decree on the Missionary Activity of the Church. Vatican Council II: Constitutions, Decrees, Declarations*, edited by Austin Flannery, 443–97. Northport, N.Y.: Costello, 1996.

————. *Gaudium et spes. Pastoral Constitution on the Church in the Modern World. Vatican Council II: Constitutions, Decrees, Declarations,* edited by Austin Flannery, 163–282. Northport, N.Y.: Costello, 1996.

————. *Lumen gentium. Dogmatic Constitution on the Church. Vatican Council II: Constitutions, Decrees, Declarations*, edited by Austin Flannery, 1–97. Northport, N.Y.: Costello, 1996.

————. *Sacrosanctum oecumenicum concilium Vaticanum II: Constitutiones, decreta, declarationes*. Vatican City: Typis Polyglottis Vaticanis, 1966.

————. *Unitatis redintegratio. Decree on Ecumenism. Vatican Council II: Constitutions, Decrees, Declarations,* edited by Austin Flannery, 499–523. Northport, N.Y.: Costello, 1996.

CLASSICS OF ECCLESIOLOGY

The following list is restricted to works published before 1930.

Adam, Karl. *The Spirit of Catholicism.* 1924. Reprinted with an introduction by Robert A. Krieg. New York: Crossroad, 1997.

Bellarminus, Robertus. *De controversiis christianae fidei.* In *Opera omnia,* edited by Justinus Fèvre, 12 vols. Paris: L. Vivès, 1870–74.

Billot, Ludovicus. *De ecclesia Christi.* 5th ed. Rome: Gregoriana, 1927.

Capocci, Giacomo (James of Viterbo). *Le plus ancien traité de l'Église: Jacques de Viterbe, De regimine christiano.* Edited by H.-X. Arquillière. Paris: Beauchesne, 1926.

Franzelin, Johannes B. *Theses de ecclesia Christi.* Rome: Ex Typographia Polyglotta S.C. de Propaganda Fide, 1887. 2nd ed., 1907.

Greá, D. Adrien. *L'Église et sa divine constitution.* 1885. New edition by Gaston Fontaine. Tournai: Casterman, 1965.

Giles of Rome (Egidio Colonna). *De ecclesiastica potestate.* Weimar: Böhnaus, 1929. English translation by R. W. Dyson, *Giles of Rome on Ecclesiastical Power: The* De ecclesiastica potestate *of Aegidius Romanus.* Woodbridge, Suffolk: Boydell, 1986.

Jean (Quidort) de Paris. *De potestate regia et papali.* Text reproduced in *Jean de Paris et l'ecclésiologie au XIIIe siècle,* by Jean Leclercq. Paris: J. Vrin, 1942. English version: *On Royal and Papal Power.* Translation with introduction by Arthur P. Monahan. New York: Columbia University, 1974.

Möhler, Johann Adam. *Die Einheit in der Kirche: Oder, Das Prinzip des Katholicismus.* New edition by J. R. Geiselmann. Cologne: Hegner, 1957. French translation: *L'unité dans l'Église.* Unam Sanctam, no. 2. Paris: Cerf, 1938. English translation: *Unity in the Church or the Principle of Catholicism: Presented in the Spirit of the Church Fathers of the First Three Centuries.* Edited and translated by Peter C. Erb. Washington, D.C.: Catholic University of America, 1996.

Passaglia, Carlo. *De ecclesia Christi.* 2 vols. Regensburg: G. J. Manz, 1853–56.

Schrader, Clemens. *De unitate Romana.* Freiburg: Herder, 1862.

Turrecremata, Johannes de. *Summa de ecclesia.* Rome, 1489. Venice: Apud M. Tramezinum, 1561. English Translation: John of Torquemada, *The Antiquity of the Church.* Annotated text and commentary by William E. Maguire. Washington, D.C.: Catholic University of America, 1957.

HISTORY OF ECCLESIOLOGY

Other aspects of the history of ecclesiology can be found in section 2, Survey Articles.

*Bouyer, Louis. *The Church of God: Body of Christ and Temple of the Holy Spirit*, pp. 3–155. Chicago: Franciscan Herald, 1982.

*Congar, Yves M.-J. *L'Église de S. Augustin à l'époque moderne.* Paris: Cerf, 1970. This is a French version of his contribution to *Handbuch der Dogmengeschichte* (see below).

Gratsch, Edward J. *Where Peter Is: A Survey of Ecclesiology.* Staten Island, N.Y.: Alba House, 1975.

Handbuch der Dogmengeschichte. Vol. 3, fascicles a–d. "Die Lehre von der Kirche," by P. V. Dias, P. T. Camelot, and Y. M.-J. Congar. Freiburg: Herder, 1970–74.

Jay, Eric G. *The Church: Its Changing Image through Twenty Centuries.* Atlanta: John Knox, 1980.

---

*An asterisk before a title indicates that the work is of broad interest and serves as a good introduction to the topic.

8

NEW TESTAMENT

Banks, Robert J. *Paul's Idea of Community*. Grand Rapids, Mich.: Wm. B. Eerdmans, 1980.

Benoit, Pierre. *Exégèse et théologie*. 3 vols. Paris: Cerf, 1961–68.

Birkey, Del. *The House Church: A Model for Renewing the Church*. Scottdale, Pa.: Herald, 1988.

Bourke, Myles M. "Reflections on Church Order in the New Testament." *Catholic Biblical Quarterly* 30 (1968): 493–511.

Branick, Vincent P. *The House Church in the Writings of Paul*. Collegeville, Minn.: Liturgical Press, 1989.

Brown, Raymond E. *Biblical Reflections on Crises Facing the Church*. New York: Paulist, 1975.

———. *The Churches the Apostles Left Behind*. New York: Paulist, 1984.

———. *The Community of the Beloved Disciple*. New York: Paulist, 1979.

Brown, Raymond E., and John P. Meier. *Antioch and Rome: New Testament Cradles of Catholic Christianity*. New York: Paulist, 1983.

Burtchaell, James T. *From Synagogue to Church: Public Services and Offices in the Earliest Christian Communities.* Cambridge, Mass. and New York: Cambridge University Press, 1992.

Campenhausen, Hans von. *Ecclesiastical Authority and Spiritual Power in the Church of the First Three Centuries.* Stanford, Calif.: Stanford University, 1969.

Cerfaux, Lucien. *The Church in the Theology of St. Paul.* New York: Herder and Herder, 1959.

Cody, Aelred. "The Foundation of the Church: Biblical Criticism for Ecumenical Discussion." *Theological Studies* 34 (1973): 3–18.

Cullmann, Oscar. *The State in the New Testament.* New York: Scribner, 1956.

Cwiekowski, Frederick J. *The Beginnings of the Church.* New York and Mahwah, N.J.: Paulist, 1988.

Davies, John G. *The Early Christian Church.* New York: Holt, Rinehart and Winston, 1965.

Donfried, Karl P., ed. *The Romans Debate.* Revised and expanded ed. Peabody, Mass.: Hendrickson, 1991.

Dunn, James D. G. *Unity and Diversity in the New Testament.* Philadelphia: Westminster, 1977.

Ferguson, Everett. *The Church of Christ: A Biblical Ecclesiology for Today.* Grand Rapids, Mich.: Wm. B. Eerdmans, 1996.

Fiorenza, Francis S. *Foundational Theology: Jesus and the Church,* chaps. 3–6. New York: Crossroad, 1984.

Gager, John G. *Kingdom and Community: The Social World of Early Christianity.* Englewood Cliffs, N.J.: Prentice-Hall, 1975.

Giblet, Jean, et al. *The Birth of the Church.* Staten Island, N.Y.: Alba House, 1968.

Guillet, Jacques. *Entre Jésus et l'Église.* Paris: Seuil, 1985.

Guitton, Jean. *The Church and the Gospel*. Westminster, Md.: Newman, 1961.

Harrington, Daniel J. *God's People in Christ: New Testament Perspectives on the Church and Judaism*. Philadelphia: Fortress, 1980.

*————. *Light of All Nations: Studies on the Church in New Testament Research*. Wilmington, Del.: Michael Glazier, 1982.

Hoffmann, Joseph. "L'Église et son origine." In *Initiation à la pratique de la théologie*, edited by B. Lauret and F. Refoulé, 3:55–141. Paris: Cerf, 1983.

Holmberg, Bengt. *Paul and Power: The Structure of Authority and Power in the Primitive Church as Reflected in the Pauline Epistles*. Philadelphia: Fortress, 1980.

Johnson, Luke K. *Decision Making in the Church*. Philadelphia: Fortress, 1983.

Karrer, Otto. *Peter and the Church: An Examination of Cullmann's Thesis*. New York: Herder and Herder, 1963.

Käsemann, Ernst. *Essays on New Testament Themes*. Naperville, Ill.: Allenson; London: SCM, 1964.

————. *New Testament Questions for Today*. Philadelphia: Fortress, 1963; London: SCM, 1969.

Kelber, Werner H. *The Oral and the Written Gospel*. Philadelphia: Fortress, 1983.

Knox, John. *The Early Church and the Coming Great Church*. New York: Abingdon, 1955.

Lohfink, Gerhard. *Jesus and Community: The Social Dimension of Christian Faith*. New York: Paulist; Philadelphia: Fortress, 1984.

Lohse, Eduard. *The First Christians: Their Beginnings, Writings, and Beliefs*. Philadelphia: Fortress, 1983.

MacDonald, Margaret Y. *The Pauline Churches: A Socio-Historical Study of Institutionalization in the Pauline and Deutero-Pauline Writings.* Cambridge: Cambridge University, 1988.

Malherbe, Abraham. *Social Aspects of Early Christianity.* Baton Rouge: Louisiana State University, 1977.

Martin, Ralph P. *The Family and the Fellowship: New Testament Images of the Church.* Grand Rapids, Mich.: Wm. B. Eerdmans, 1980.

McKelvey, R. J. *The New Temple: The Church in the New Testament.* London: Oxford University, 1969.

Meeks, Wayne A. *The First Urban Christians: The Social World of the Apostle Paul.* New Haven, Conn.: Yale University, 1983.

Minear, Paul S. *Images of the Church in the New Testament.* Philadelphia: Westminster, 1960.

Osiek, Carolyn, and David L. Balch. *Families in the New Testament World: Households and House Churches.* Louisville, Ky.: Westminster John Knox, 1997.

Schlier, Heinrich. "Ekklesiologie des Neuen Testaments." In *Mysterium salutis*, edited by Johannes Feiner and Magnus Löhrer, 4/1:101–221. Einsiedeln: Benziger, 1972. Extensive bibliography.

————. *Die Zeit der Kirche: Exegetische Aufsätze und Vorträge.* Freiburg: Herder, 1962.

Schmidt, Karl L. *The Church: Bible Key Words from Kittel.* New York: Harper, 1951.

*Schnackenburg, Rudolf. *The Church in the New Testament.* New York: Herder and Herder, 1965.

————. *God's Rule and Kingdom.* New York: Herder and Herder, 1963.

Schweizer, Eduard. *Church Order in the New Testament*. Naperville, Ill.: Allenson, 1961.

Segovia, Fernando F., ed. *Discipleship in the New Testament*. Philadelphia: Fortress, 1985.

Senior, Donald, and Carroll Stuhlmueller. *The Biblical Foundations for Mission*. Maryknoll, N.Y.: Orbis, 1983.

Stanley, David M. *The Apostolic Church in the New Testament*. Westminster, Md.: Newman, 1965.

Stendahl, Krister. "Kirche, II. Im Urchristentum." In *Religion in Geschichte und Gegenwart*. 3rd ed. Vol. 1, cols. 1279–1304. Tübingen: J. C. B. Mohr, 1959.

Theissen, Gerd. *Sociology of Early Palestinian Christianity*. Philadelphia: Fortress, 1977.

Verbraken, Patrick. *The Beginnings of the Church*. Glen Rock, N.J.: Paulist, 1968.

*Warnach, Viktor. "Church " In *Sacramentum Verbi,* 1:101–16. New York: Herder and Herder, 1970.

Zehnle, Richard. *The Making of the Christian Church*. Notre Dame, Ind.: Fides, 1969.

THE PATRISTIC ERA

Bardy, Gustave. *La théologie de l'Église, de S. Clément de Rome à S. Irénée.* Unam Sanctam, no. 13. Paris: Cerf, 1945.

————. *La théologie de l'Église, de S. Irénée au Concile de Nicée.* Unam Sanctam, no. 14. Paris: Cerf, 1947.

Bowe, Barbara. *A Church in Crisis: Ecclesiology and Paraenesis in Clement of Rome.* Minneapolis: Fortress, 1988.

Campenhausen, Hans von. *Ecclesiastical Authority and Spiritual Power in the Church of the First Three Centuries.* Stanford, Calif.: Stanford University, 1969.

Colson, Jean. *Les fonctions ecclésiales aux deux premiers siècles.* Paris: Desclée De Brouwer, 1965.

Daniélou, Jean, and Herbert Vorgrimler, eds. *Sentire Ecclesiam: Festgabe H. Rahner.* Freiburg: Herder, 1961. Historical studies.

Delahaye, Karl. *Ecclesia Mater chez les Pères des trois premiers siècles.* Unam Sanctam, no. 46. Paris: Cerf, 1964.

*Evans, Robert F. *One and Holy: The Church in Latin Patristic Thought.* London: SPCK, 1972.

Halton, Thomas. *The Church.* Wilmington, Del.: Michael Glazier, 1985.

*Hertling, Ludwig. *Communio: Church and Papacy in Early Christianity*. Introduction by Jared Wicks. Chicago: Loyola University, 1972.

Ladner, Gerhart B. *The Idea of Reform: Its Impact on Christian Thought and Action in the Age of the Fathers*. Cambridge, Mass.: Harvard University, 1959.

Lienhard, Joseph T. *The Bible, The Church, and Authority: The Canon of the Christian Bible in History and Theology*. Collegeville, Minn.: Liturgical Press, 1995.

McShane, Philip A. *La romanitas et le pape Léon le Grand: L'apport culturel des institutions impériales à la formation des structures ecclésiastiques*. Tournai: Desclée; Montreal: Bellarmin, 1979.

Mersch, Émile. *The Whole Christ: The Historical Development of the Doctrine of the Mystical Body*. Milwaukee, Wis.: Bruce, 1938.

Murray, Robert. *Symbols of Church and Kingdom: A Study in Early Syriac Tradition*. Cambridge: Cambridge University, 1975.

Plumpe, Joseph C. *Mater Ecclesia: An Inquiry into the Concept of the Church as Mother in Early Christianity*. Washington, D.C.: Catholic University of America, 1943.

Rahner, Hugo. *Symbole der Kirche: Die Ekklesiologie der Väter*. Salzburg: Müller, 1964.

Rankin, David. *Tertullian and the Church*. New York: Cambridge University, 1995.

Scazzoso, Piero. *Introduzione alla ecclesiologia di S. Basilio*. Milan: Università Cattolica del S. Cuore, 1975.

ST. AUGUSTINE

The works given here are in addition to the items referred to in the preceding section.

Balthasar, Hans Urs von. *Augustinus, Das Antlitz der Kirche*. Einsiedeln: Benziger, 1955. French translation: *S. Augustin: Le visage de l'Église. Textes choisis et présentés*. Unam Sanctam, no. 31. Paris: Cerf, 1958.

Bavel, T. J. van. "What Kind of Church Do You Want? The Breadth of Augustine's Ecclesiology." *Louvain Studies* 7 (1979): 147-71.

Bonner, Gerald. "The Church and the Eucharist in the Theology of Saint Augustine." *Sobornost* 7 (1978): 448-61.

Borgomeo, Pasquale. *L'Église de ce temps dans la prédication de St. Augustin*. Paris: Études Augustiniennes, 1972.

Desjardins, R. "Le Christ *sponsus* et l'Église *sponsa* chez Augustin." *Bulletin de littérature ecclésiastique* 67 (1967): 241-56.

Eno, Robert. "Doctrinal Authority in St. Augustine." *Augustinian Studies* 12 (1981): 137-72.

Faul, D. "Sinners in the Holy Church: A Problem in the Ecclesiology of St. Augustine." *Studia Patristica* 9 (1966): 404-15.

*Grabowski, Stanislaus J. *The Church: An Introduction to the Theology of St. Augustine*. St. Louis, Mo.: Herder, 1957.

Hofmann, Fritz. *Der Kirchenbegriff des hl. Augustinus*. Munich: M. Hueber, 1933. Reprint, Münster: Th. Stenderhoff, 1978.

Lamirande, Émilien. *Études sur l'ecclésiologie de S. Augustin*. Ottawa: Université Saint-Paul et Université d'Ottawa, 1969.

―――. "Un siècle et demi d'études sur l'ecclésiologie de saint Augustin." *Revue des études Augustiniennes* 8 (1962): 1–125. A bibliography from 1809 to 1954.

―――. *La situation ecclésiologique des Donatistes d'après S. Augustin*. Ottawa: Université d'Ottawa, 1972.

Mondin, Battista. "Il pensiero ecclesiologico di Sant'Agostino." *Sapienza* 40 (1987): 369–91.

Ratzinger, Joseph. "Die Kirche in der Frömmigkeit des heiligen Augustinus." In *Sentire Ecclesiam: Festgabe H. Rahner*, edited by Jean Daniélou and Herbert Vorgrimler, 152–75. Freiburg: Herder, 1961.

―――. *Volk und Haus Gottes in Augustins Lehre von der Kirche*. Munich: Zink, 1954.

THE MIDDLE AGES

Alberigo, Giuseppe. *Cardinalato e Collegialità*. Florence: Vallecchi, 1969.

―――. *Chiesa conciliare: Identità e significato del conciliarismo*. Brescia: Paideia, 1981.

Arnau-García, Ramon. *San Vincente Ferrer y las eclesiologías del Cisma*. Valencia: Artes Graficas Soler, 1987.

Black, Antony. *Council and Commune: The Conciliar Movement and the Council of Basle*. London: Burns & Oates; Shepherdstown, W. Va.: Patmos, 1979.

―――. "What Was Conciliarism? Conciliar Theory in Historical Perspective." In *Authority and Power: Studies in Medieval Law and Government*, edited by Brian Tierney and Peter Linehan, 213–24. Cambridge: Cambridge University, 1980.

Blumenthal, Uta-Renate. *The Investiture Controversy: Church and Monarchy from the Ninth to the Twelfth Century*. Philadelphia: University of Pennsylvania, 1988.

Chodorow, Stanley. *Christian Political Theory and Church Politics in the Mid-Twelfth Century: The Ecclesiology of Gratian's Decretum*. Berkeley, Calif.: University of California, 1972.

Congar, Yves M.-J. "Ecclesia ab Abel." In *Abhandlungen über*

Theologie und Kirche: Festschrift für Karl Adam, edited by Marcel Reding. Düsseldorf: Patmos, 1952.

———. "L'ecclésiologie de S. Bernard." *Analecta Sacri Ordinis Cisterciensis* 9 (1953): 136–90.

———. *L'ecclésiologie du haut moyen-âge, de S. Grégoire le Grand à la désunion entre Byzance et Rome.* Paris: Cerf, 1968.

*———. *L'Église de S. Augustin à l'époque moderne.* Paris: Cerf, 1970.

Delaruelle, Étienne, et al. *L'Église au temps du Grand Schisme et de la crise conciliare.* In *Histoire de l'Église,* vol. 14. Paris: Bloud et Gay, 1962.

Franzen, August. "The Council of Constance." Concilium, no. 7, edited by Roger Aubert, 29–68. Glen Rock, N.J.: Paulist, 1965.

Heft, James. *John XXII and Papal Teaching Authority.* Lewiston, N.Y.: Edwin Mellen, 1986.

Huss, John. *Tractatus de Ecclesia.* English version: *The Church by John Huss.* Translation by David S. Schaff. New York: Scribner, 1915. Reprint, Westport, Conn.: Greenwood, 1971.

Izbicki, Thomas M. *Protector of the Faith: Johannes de Turrecremata and the Defense of the Institutional Church.* Washington, D.C.: Catholic University of America, 1981.

*Küng, Hans. *Structures of the Church.* New York: T. Nelson, 1964. Discussion of conciliarism, 268–319.

Lecler, Joseph. *Le pape ou le concile? Une interrogation de l'Église médiévale.* Lyon: Le Chalet, 1973.

Leclercq, Jean. *Jean de Paris et l'ecclésiologie au XIIIe siécle.* Paris: J. Vrin, 1942.

Lytle, Guy F., ed. *Reform and Authority in the Medieval and Reformation Church.* Washington, D.C.: Catholic University of America, 1981.

Oakley, Francis. *Council over Pope? Towards a Provisional Ecclesiology.* New York: Herder and Herder, 1969.

———. "The 'New Conciliarism' and Its Implications: A Problem of History and Hermeneutics." *Journal of Ecumenical Studies* 8 (1971): 815–40.

Pascoe, Louis B. *Jean Gerson: Principles of Church Reform.* Leiden: Brill, 1973.

Ryan, John J. *The Nature, Structure, and Function of the Church in William of Ockham.* American Academy of Religion, Studies in Religion, no. 16. Missoula, Mont.: Scholars Press, 1979.

Smith, John Holland. *The Great Schism of 1378: The Disintegration of the Papacy.* New York: Weybright & Talley, 1970.

Spinka, Matthew. *John Hus' Concept of the Church.* Princeton, N.J.: Princeton University, 1966.

Swiezawski, Stefan. *Les tribulations de l'ecclésiologie à la fin du moyen âge.* Paris: Beauchesne, 1997.

Tierney, Brian. *Foundations of Conciliar Theory: The Contributions of the Medieval Canonists from Gratian to the Great Schism.* Cambridge: Cambridge University, 1955.

———. *The Origins of Papal Infallibility (1150–1350).* Leiden: Brill, 1973.

Ullmann, Walter. *The Growth of Papal Government in the Middle Ages.* London: Methuen, 1955.

Vooght, Paul de. *Les pouvoirs du concile et l'autorité du pape au concile de Constance.* Unam Sanctam, no. 56. Paris: Cerf, 1965.

———. "The Results of Recent Historical Research on Conciliarism." In *Papal Ministry in the Church,* edited by Hans Küng, 148–57. Concilium, no. 64. New York: Herder and Herder, 1971.

ST. THOMAS AQUINAS

The following material on St. Thomas is in addition to the references given in the previous section on the Middle Ages.

Congar, Yves M.-J. *L'Église de saint Augustin à l'époque moderne.* Paris: Cerf, 1970. A discussion of the ecclesiology of St. Thomas (pp. 232–41).

————. "The Idea of the Church in St. Thomas Aquinas." In *The Mystery of the Church,* chap. 3. Baltimore: Helicon, 1960.

————. "Vision de l'Église chez Thomas d'Aquin." *Revue des sciences philosophiques et théologiques* 62 (1978): 523–42.

*Dulles, Avery. "The Church according to Thomas Aquinas." In *A Church to Believe In,* chap. 10. New York: Crossroad, 1982.

Grabmann, Martin. *Die Lehre des hl. Thomas von Aquin von der Kirche als Gotteswerk.* Regensburg: G. J. Manz, 1903.

Ménard, Étienne. *La Tradition: Révélation, Écriture, Église selon S. Thomas d'Aquin.* Paris: Desclée De Brouwer, 1964.

O'Neill, Colman. "St. Thomas on the Membership of the Church." *Vatican II: The Theological Dimension. Thomist* 27 (1963): 88–140.

Sabra, George. *Thomas Aquinas' Vision of the Church: Fundmentals of an Ecumenical Ecclesiology*. Mainz: Matthias-Grünewald, 1987.

Seckler, Max. *Das Heil in der Geschichte*. Munich: Kösel, 1964.

Useros Carretero, Manuel. *"Statuta Ecclesiae" y "Sacramenta Ecclesiae" en la eclesiología de St. Tomás*. Rome: Gregoriana, 1962.

THE REFORMATION

Avis, Paul D. *The Church in the Theology of the Reformers*. Atlanta: John Knox, 1981.

Congar, Yves M.-J. *Vraie et fausse Réforme dans l'Église*. Unam Sanctam, no. 20. Paris: Cerf, 1950. Revised edition, 1968. See chapters on the ecclesiology of Luther.

Ganoczy, Alexandre. *Calvin: Théologien de l'Église et du ministère*. Unam Sanctam, no. 48. Paris: Cerf, 1964.

Gassmann, Benno. *Ecclesia Reformata: Die Kirche in den reformierten Bekenntnisschriften*. Freiburg: Herder, 1968.

*Hendrix, Scott H. *Luther and the Papacy: Stages in a Reformation Conflict*. Philadelphia: Fortress, 1981.

Lienhard, Marc. *L'Évangile et l'Église chez Luther*. Paris: Cerf, 1989.

Manns, Peter, and Harding Meyer, eds., in collaboration with Carter Lindberg and Harry McSorley. *Luther's Ecumenical Significance: An Interconfessional Consultation*. Philadelphia: Fortress; New York: Paulist, 1984. See articles on Luther's ecclesiology by H. Vajta and H.-W. Scheele (pp. 111–58).

McDonnell, Kilian. *John Calvin: The Church and the Eucharist*. Princeton, N.J.: Princeton University, 1967.

Meyer, Harding, and Heinz Schütte. "The Concept of the Church in the Augsburg Confession." In *Confessing One Faith: A Joint Commentary on the Augsburg Confession by Lutheran and Catholic Theologians*, edited by George W. Forell and James F. McCue, 173–201. Minneapolis: Augsburg, 1982.

*Milner, Benjamin C. *Calvin's Doctrine of the Church*. Leiden: Brill, 1970.

*Minnich, Nelson H. *Catholic Reformation: Council, Churchmen, Controversies*. Brookfield, Vt.: Variorum, 1993.

Mollat, G. *The Popes at Avignon 1305–1378*. London: Thomas Nelson, 1963.

Olin, John C. *The Catholic Reformation: Savonarola to Ignatius Loyola. Reform in the Church 1495–1540*. New York: Harper & Row, 1969.

———. *Catholic Reform: From Cardinal Ximenes to the Council of Trent 1495–1563*. New York: Fordham University, 1990.

Preus, Herman A. *The Communion of Saints: A Study of the Origin and Development of Luther's Doctrine of the Church*. Minneapolis: Augsburg, 1948.

Torrance, Thomas F. *Kingdom and Church: A Study in the Theology of the Reformation*. Edinburgh: Oliver & Boyd, 1956. On Luther, Butzer, Calvin.

Wicks, Jared. *Cajetan Responds: A Reader in Reformation Controversy*. Washington, D.C.: Catholic University of America, 1978.

14

THE SEVENTEENTH THROUGH THE NINETEENTH CENTURIES

Alberigo, Giuseppe. *Lo sviluppo della dottrina sui poteri nella chiesa universale: momenti essenziali tra il XVI e XIX secolo*. Rome: Herder, 1964.

At, Jean-Antoine. *Les apologistes français au XIXe siècle*. Paris: Bloud et Barral, 1898.

Bárczay, Gyula. *Ecclesia semper reformanda: Eine Untersuchung zum Kirchenbegriff des 19. Jahrhunderts*. Zurich: EVZ, 1969.

Chaillet, Pierre, ed. *L'Église est une: Hommage à Möhler*. Paris: Bloud et Gay, 1939.

Costigan, Richard F. *Rohrbacher and the Ecclesiology of Ultramontanism*. Rome: Gregoriana, 1980.

Facoltà teologica interregionale Milano. *L'ecclesiologia dal Vaticano I al Vaticano II*. Brescia: La Scuola, 1973. Articles by A. Antón, G. Thils, C. Vagaggini, U. Betti, and others.

Hardon, John. "Robert Bellarmine's Concept of the Church." In *Studies in Medieval Culture*, edited by J. Sommerfeldt, 2:120–27. Kalamazoo, Mich.: Western Michigan Press, 1966.

*Himes, Michael J. *Ongoing Incarnation: Johann Adam Möhler and the Beginnings of Modern Ecclesiology*. New York: Crossroad, 1997.

Hocedez, Edgar. *Histoire de la théologie au XIXe siècle*. 3 vols. Brussels: Universelle; Paris: Desclée De Brouwer, 1948.

Martimort, Aimé-Georges. *Le Gallicanisme*. Paris: Presses universitaires de France, 1973.

Martin, Victor. *Les origines du Gallicanisme*. 2 vols. Paris: Bloud et Gay, 1939.

*Miller, Edward J. *John Henry Newman on the Idea of Church*. Shepherdstown, W. Va.: Patmos, 1987.

*Nédoncelle, Maurice, Roger Aubert, Y. M.-J. Congar, et al. *L'ecclésiologie au XIXe siècle*. Unam Sanctam, no. 34. Paris:

O'Meara, Thomas F. "Beyond 'Hierarchology': Johann Adam Möhler and Yves Congar." In *The Legacy of the Tübingen School: The Relevance of Nineteenth Century Theology for the Twenty-First Century*, edited by Donald J. Dietrich and Michael J. Himes, 173–91. New York: Crossroad, 1997.

Palmer, William. *A Treatise on the Church of Christ*. 2nd ed. 2 vols. New York: Appleton, 1841. Anglo-Catholic.

Tavard, George H. *The Quest for Catholicity: A Study in Anglicanism*. New York: Herder and Herder, 1964.

Thils, Gustave. *Les notes de l'Église dans l'apologétique catholique depuis la Réforme*. Gembloux: J. Duculot, 1937.

15

VATICAN COUNCIL I

On this topic also see section 35, The Papacy, and section 38, Infallibility.

*Aubert, Roger. "L'ecclésiologie au Concile du Vatican." In *Le Concile et les Conciles*. Chevetogne: Chevetogne, 1960.

———. *Vatican I*. Paris: Orante, 1964.

Aubert, Roger, Michel Guéret, and Paul Tombeur, eds. *Concilium Vaticanum I: Concordance, index, listes de fréquence, tables comparatives*. Louvain: Cétedoc, 1977.

Betti, Umberto. *La costituzione dommatica: 'Pastor Aeternus' del Concilio Vaticano I*. Rome: Antonianum, 1961.

Broderick, John F. *Documents of Vatican I, 1869–1870*. Collegeville, Minn.: Liturgical Press, 1971.

*Butler, Cuthbert. *The Vatican Council*. Reissue. Westminster, Md.: Newman, 1962.

Dejaifve, Georges. "First among Bishops." *Eastern Churches Quarterly* 14 (1961): 2–25.

———. *Pape et évêques au premier concile du Vatican*. Paris: Desclée De Brouwer, 1961.

———. "Ex sese, non autem ex consensu ecclesiae." *Salesianum* 24 (1962): 283–97. Also in *Symposium international de théologie dogmatique fondamentale (Louvain, 1961)*. Turin: Società editrice internationale, 1962.

Fessler, J. *The True and False Infallibility of the Popes*. New York: Catholic Publication Society, 1875.

Granderath, Theodor. *Constitutiones dogmaticae sacrosancti oecumenici Concilii Vaticani ex ipsis actis explicatae atque illustratae*. Freiburg: Herder, 1892.

———. *Geschichte des Vatikanischen Konzils von seiner ersten Anküngdigung bis seiner Vertragung*. Edited by Konrad Kirch. 3 vols. Freiburg: Herder, 1903–6. French version: *Histoire du concile du Vatican, depuis sa premiére annonce jusqu'á sa prorogation*. 4 vols. Brussels: A. Dewit, 1907–14.

Hasler, August B. *Pius IX (1846-1878), päptsliche Unfehlbarkeit, und I. Vatikanisches Konzil: Dogmatisierung und Durchsetzung einer Ideologie*. 2 vols. Stuttgart: Anton Hiersemann, 1977. A shorter version in English: *How the Pope Became Infallible: Pius IX and the Politics of Persuasion*. Garden City, N.Y.: Doubleday, 1981.

Hennesey, James. *The First Council of the Vatican: The American Experience*. New York: Herder and Herder, 1963.

Horst, Fidelis van der. *Das Schema über die Kirche auf dem I. Vatikanischen Konzil*. Paderborn: Bonifacius, 1963.

Newman, John Henry. "A Letter Addressed to His Grace the Duke of Norfolk." In *Newman and Gladstone: The Vatican Decrees*, edited by A. S. Ryan. Notre Dame, Ind.: University of Notre Dame, 1962.

Schatz, Klaus. *Vatikanum I (1869-1870)*. Vol. 1, *Vor der Eröffnung*. Vol. 2, *Von der Eröffnung bis zur Konstitution "Dei Filius."* Vol. 3, *Unfehlbarkeitsdiskussion und Rezeption*. Paderborn: F. Schöningh, 1992, 1993, 1994.

Thils, Gustave. *Primauté pontificale et prérogatives épiscopales: "Potestas Ordinaria" au concile du Vatican*. Louvain: É. Warny, 1961.

*————. *La primauté pontificale: La doctrine de Vatican I*. Gembloux: J. Duculot, 1972.

Torrell, Jean-Pierre. *La théologie de l'épiscopat au premier Concile du Vatican*. Unam Sanctam, no. 37. Paris: Cerf, 1961.

16

VATICAN COUNCIL II

The following two books are most useful in working with the Council documents.

Delhaye, Philippe, Michel Guéret, and Paul Tombeur, eds. *Concilium Vaticanum II: Concordance, index, listes de fréquence, tables comparatives.* Louvain: Cétedoc, 1974.

Ochoa, Xaverius, ed. *Index verborum cum documentis Concilii Vaticani Secundi.* Rome: Commentarium pro Religiosis, 1967.

• • •

Acerbi, Antonio. *Due ecclesiologie: Ecclesiologia giuridica ed ecclesiologia di comunione nella "Lumen gentium."* Bologna: Dehoniane, 1975.

Alberigo, Giuseppe, ed. *L'ecclesiologia del Vaticano II: Dinamismi e prospettive.* Bologna: Dehoniane, 1981. Articles by G. Alberigo, P. Fransen, H. J. Pottmeyer, and others. French version: *Les Églises après Vatican II: Dynamisme et prospective.* Paris: Beauchesne, 1981.

Alberigo, Giuseppe, Jean-Pierre Jossua, and Joseph A. Komonchak, eds. *The Reception of Vatican II.* Washington, D.C.: Catholic University of America, 1987. Articles by G. Alberigo, J. A. Komonchak, H. J. Pottmeyer, G. Gutiérrez, and others.

*Alberigo, Giuseppe, and Joseph A. Komonchak, eds. *History of Vatican II: Volume I: Announcing and Preparing Vatican Council II*. Maryknoll, N.Y.: Orbis; Leuven: Peeters, 1996. Volume II (1997) is entitled: *The Formation of the Council's Identity: First Period and Intersession October 1962–September 1963*. Three other volumes are planned.

Alberigo, Giuseppe, and Franca Magistretti. *Constitutionis dogmaticae Lumen gentium synopsis historica*. Bologna: Istituto per le scienze religiose, 1975.

Antón, Angel. "Postconciliar Ecclesiology: Expectations, Results, and Prospects for the Future." In *Vatican II: Assessments and Perspectives: Twenty-Five Years After (1962–1987)*, edited by René Latourelle, 1:407–38. New York: Paulist, 1988.

Baraúna, Guilherme, ed. *L'Église de Vatican II*. 3 vols. Unam Sanctam, no. 51 a, b, c. Paris: Cerf, 1966. Italian version: *La Chiesa del Vaticano II*. Florence: Vallecchi, 1965. German version: *De Ecclesia: Beiträge zur Konstitution über die Kirche des II. Vatikanischen Konzils*. Freiburg: Herder, 1966.

Barth, Karl. *Ad Limina Apostolorum*. Richmond, Va.: John Knox, 1968.

Berkouwer, Gerrit C. *The Second Vatican Council and the New Catholicism*. Grand Rapids, Mich.: Wm. B. Eerdmans, 1965.

Butler, Christopher. *The Theology of Vatican II*. Rev. ed. Westminster, Md.: Christian Classics, 1981.

Congar, Yves M.-J. *Le concile de Vatican II–son Église: Peuple de Dieu et Corps du Christ*. Paris: Beauchesne, 1984.

———. "Sur la trilogie: Prophète-Roi-Prêtre." *Revue des sciences philosophiques et théologiques* 67 (1983): 97–114.

Coste, René. *L'Église et les défis du monde: La dynamique de Vatican II*. Paris: Nouvelle Cité, 1986.

Cullmann, Oscar. *Vatican II: The New Direction*. New York: Harper & Row, 1968.

Dejaifve, Georges. *Un tournant décisif de l'ecclésiologie à Vatican II.* Paris: Beauchesne, 1978.

Doyle, Dennis M. *The Church Emerging from Vatican II: A Popular Approach to Contemporary Catholicism.* Mystic, Conn.: Twenty-Third, 1992.

Dulles, Avery. *The Dimensions of the Church.* Westminster, Md.: Newman, 1967.

Fagin, Gerald M., ed. *Vatican II: Open Questions and New Horizons.* Wilmington, Del.: Michael Glazier, 1984. Articles by A. Dulles, G. Lindbeck, S. Duffy, G. Baum, and F. Cardman.

Hastings, Adrian, ed. *Modern Catholicism: Vatican II and After.* London: SPCK; New York: Oxford University, 1991.

Holstein, Henri. *Hiérarchie et Peuple de Dieu d'après "Lumen Gentium."* Paris: Beauchesne, 1970.

Istituto Paolo VI. *Giovanni Battista Montini Arcivescovo di Milano e il Concilio Ecumenico Vaticano II: Preparazione e primo periodo.* Brescia: Istituto Paolo VI, 1985.

———. *Paolo VI e i problemi ecclesiologici al Concilio.* Brescia: Istituto Paolo VI, 1989.

———. *Paolo VI e il rapporto chiesa-mondo al Concilio.* Brescia: Istituto Paolo VI, 1991.

Jedin, Hubert, "The Second Vatican Council." In *History of the Church*, vol. 10, *The Church in the Modern World,* edited by H. Jedin, K. Repgen, and J. Dolan, 96–151 and bibliography, 814–17. New York: Crossroad, 1981.

Klinger, Elmar, and Klaus Wittstadt, eds. *Glaube im Prozess: Christsein nach dem II. Vatikanum. Für Karl Rahner.* Freiburg: Herder, 1984. Articles on Vatican II by M.-D. Chenu, Y. M.-J. Congar, G. Alberigo, H. Fries, P. Fransen, and others.

Kloppenburg, Bonaventure. *The Ecclesiology of Vatican II.* Chicago: Franciscan Herald, 1970.

Kobler, John F. *Vatican II and Phenomenology: Reflections on the Life-World of the Church.* Dordrecht: M. Nijhoff, 1985.

————. *Vatican II, Theophany, and the Phenomenon of Man: The Council's Pastoral Servant Leader Theology for the Third Millennium.* New York: Peter Lang, 1991.

Lindbeck, George. *The Future of Roman Catholic Theology.* Philadelphia: Fortress, 1970.

McNamara, Kevin. *Vatican II: The Constitution on the Church. A Theological and Pastoral Commentary.* Chicago: Franciscan Herald, 1968.

Miller, John H., ed. *Vatican II: An Interfaith Appraisal.* Notre Dame, Ind.: University of Notre Dame, 1966. For matter pertaining to *Lumen Gentium,* see the contributions of J. Medina Estevez, H. de Lubac, C. Moeller, G. Philips, Y. M.-J. Congar, C. Colombo, G. Lindbeck, B. Häring, and B. Ahern.

*Philips, Gérard. *L'Église et son mystére au IIe Concile du Vatican.* 2 vols. Paris: Desclée, 1967.

*Philips, Gérard, Aloys Grillmeier, Karl Rahner, Ferdinand Klostermann, Friedrich Wulf, Otto Semmelroth, and Joseph Ratzinger. "Dogmatic Constitution on the Church." In *Commentary on the Documents of Vatican II,* edited by Herbert Vorgrimler, 1:105–305. New York: Herder and Herder, 1967.

Richard, Lucien, et al., eds. *Vatican II: The Unfinished Agenda. A Look to the Future.* New York and Mahwah, N.J.: Paulist, 1987. Articles by L. Richard, K. Rahner, J. O'Malley, and others.

Routhier, Gilles. *La recéption d'un concile.* Paris: Cerf, 1993.

Schlink, Edmund. *After the Council.* Philadelphia: Fortress, 1968.

Schner, George P., ed. *The Church Renewed: The Documents of Vatican II Reconsidered.* Lanham, Md.: University Press of America, 1986.

Schönmetzer, Adolfus, ed. *Acta congressus internationalis de theologia concilii Vaticani secundi.* Vatican City: Typis Polyglottis Vaticanis, 1968. Articles by H. Schauf, H. de Lubac, K. Rahner, F. A. Sullivan, and others.

Shook, L. K., ed. *Theology of Renewal.* 2 vols. New York: Herder and Herder, 1968.

Stacpoole, Alberic, ed. *Vatican II Revisited by Those Who Were There.* Minneapolis: Winston, 1986.

Wojtyla, Karol (John Paul II). *Sources of Renewal: The Implementation of Vatican II.* San Francisco: Harper & Row, 1980.

For the history of the council, consult also the well-known works of Xavier Rynne, Henri Fesquet, Antoine Wenger, Michael Novak, Robert B. Kaiser, et al.

TRENDS IN TWENTIETH-CENTURY ROMAN CATHOLIC ECCLESIOLOGY

Adolfs, Robert. *The Grave of God: Has the Church a Future?* London: Burns & Oates, 1967.

Antón, Angel. *El misterio de la Iglesia: Evolución histórica de las ideas eclesiológicas.* Madrid: Biblioteca de Autores Cristianos and Editorial Católica; Toledo: Estudio Teologico de San Ildefonso, 1986–87.

Bacik, James J. *Tensions in the Church: Facing the Challenges, Seizing the Opportunities.* Kansas City, Mo.: Sheed & Ward, 1993.

Baum, Gregory. *The Credibility of the Church Today.* New York: Herder and Herder, 1968.

Braxton, Edward K. *The Wisdom Community.* New York: Paulist, 1980.

Broucker, José de, ed. *The Suenens Dossier.* Notre Dame, Ind.: Fides, 1970.

Congar, Yves M.-J. "Situation ecclésiologique au moment de 'Ecclesiam suam' et passage à une Église dans l'itinéraire des hommes." In *Ecclesiam suam: Première lettre encyclique de Paul*

VI, 79–102. Brescia: Istituto Paolo VI, 1982. Other articles by R. Aubert, G. Colombo, and others.

Donovan, Daniel. *The Church as Idea and Fact*. Wilmington, Del.: Michael Glazier, 1988.

*Dulles, Avery. *A Church to Believe In*. New York: Crossroad, 1982.

———. "A Half-Century of Ecclesiology." *Theological Studies* 50 (1989): 419–42.

*———. *The Reshaping of Catholicism: Current Challenges in the Theology of the Church*. San Francisco: Harper & Row, 1988.

———. *The Resilient Church*. Garden City, N.Y.: Doubleday, 1977.

Eagan, Joseph F. *The Church in the Third Millennium*. Kansas City, Mo.: Sheed & Ward, 1995.

Fahey, Michael A. "Church." In *Systematic Theology: Roman Catholic Perspectives*, edited by Francis Schüssler Fiorenza and John P. Galvin, 2:3–74. Minneapolis: Fortress, 1991.

Fouilloux, Etienne. *Les catholiques et l'unité chrétienne du XIXe siècle au XXe siècle*. Paris: Centurion, 1982.

Frisque, Jean. "L'ecclésiologie au XXe siècle." In *Bilan de la théologie du XXe siècle*, edited by Robert Vander Gucht and Herbert Vorgrimler, 2:412–56. Tournai: Casterman, 1970.

Giussani, Luigi. *Why The Church?* Montreal: McGill-Queen's University, 1998.

Grootaers, Jan. *De Vatican I à Jean Paul II: Le grand tournant de l'Église Catholique*. Paris: Centurion, 1981.

Hebblethwaite, Peter. *The Runaway Church: Post-Conciliar Growth or Decline*. New York: Seabury, 1975.

Hegy, Pierre, ed. *The Church in the Nineties: Its Legacy, Its Future*. Collegeville, Minn.: Liturgical Press, 1993.

Hoffman, Virginia. *Birthing a Living Church*. New York: Crossroad, 1988.

*Jaki, Stanislaus. *Les tendances nouvelles de l'ecclésiologie*. Rome: Herder, 1957.

Kaitholil, George. *Church: The Sacrament of Christ. Patristic Vision and Modern Theology*. Staten Island, N.Y.: Alba House, 1998.

Kasper, Walter. *Theology and Church*. New York: Crossroad, 1989.

Komonchak, Joseph A. *Foundations in Ecclesiology*. A supplementary issue of *Lonergan Workshop Journal*, vol. 11 (1995).

Küng, Hans. *On Being a Christian*. Garden City, N.Y.: Doubleday, 1976.

Lee, Bernard. *The Becoming of the Church: A Process Theology*. New York: Paulist, 1974.

Légaut, Marcel. *Mutation de l'Église et conversion personnelle*. Paris: Aubier Montaigne, 1975.

Lennan, Richard. *The Ecclesiology of Karl Rahner*. New York and Oxford: Clarendon, 1995.

MacDonald, Timothy I. *The Ecclesiology of Yves Congar: Foundational Themes*. Lanham, Md.: University Press of America, 1984.

McBrien, Richard. *Church: The Continuing Quest*. Paramus, N.J.: Newman, 1970.

————. *Do We Need the Church?* New York: Harper & Row, 1969.

————. *Responses to 101 Questions on the Church*. New York and Mahwah, N.J.: Paulist, 1996.

————. *Who Is a Catholic?* Denville, N.J.: Dimension Books, 1967.

McCarthy, Timothy G. *The Catholic Tradition: The Church in the Twentieth Century*. 2nd ed. Chicago: Loyola, 1997.

Ménard, Étienne. *L'ecclésiologie: Hier et aujourd'hui*. Bruges: Desclée De Brouwer, 1966.

Minnerath, Roland. *Le droit de l'Église à la liberté du Syllabus à Vatican II*. Paris: Beauchesne, 1982.

Mondin, G. Battista. *Le nuove ecclesiologie*. Rome: Paoline, 1980.

Nadeau, Marie Thérèse. *Foi de l'Église: Evolution d'une formule*. Paris: Beauchesne, 1988.

O'Dea, Thomas F. *The Catholic Crisis*. Boston: Beacon, 1968.

O'Donovan, Leo J., et al. "A Changing Ecclesiology in a Changing Church: A Symposium on Development in the Ecclesiology of Karl Rahner." *Theological Studies* 38/4 (1977): 736–62. Articles by J. P. Schineller, J. P. Galvin, and M. A. Fahey.

Pallath, Paul, ed. *The Church and Its Most Basic Element*. Rome: Herder, 1995.

Pelchat, Marc: *L'Église mystère de communion: L'ecclésiologie dans l'oeuvre de Henri de Lubac*. Montreal: Paulines, 1988.

Preston, Geoffrey. *Faces of the Church: Meditations on a Mystery and Its Images*. Grand Rapids, Mich.: Wm. B. Eerdmans, 1997.

Rahner, Karl. *The Christian of the Future*. New York: Herder and Herder, 1967.

―――. *The Church After the Council*. New York: Herder and Herder, 1966.

―――. *The Shape of the Church to Come*. New York: Seabury, 1974.

*―――. *Theological Investigations*. New York: Crossroad. Especially vols. 2, 5, 6, 10, 12, 14, 17, and 20.

―――. *Theology of Pastoral Action*. New York: Herder and Herder, 1968.

Ratzinger, Joseph. *The Meaning of Christian Brotherhood*. San Francisco: Ignatius, 1993.

————. *Principles of Catholic Theology: Building Stones in a Fundamental Theology.* San Francisco: Ignatius, 1987.

————. *Salt of the Earth: The Church at the End of the Millennium. An Interview with Peter Seewald.* San Francisco: Ignatius, 1997.

Ratzinger, Joseph, with Vittorio Messori. *The Ratzinger Report: An Exclusive Interview on the State of the Church.* San Francisco: Ignatius, 1985.

Rikhof, Herwi. *The Concept of the Church.* London: Sheed & Ward; Shepherdstown, W. Va.: Patmos, 1981.

Ruether, Rosemary Radford. *The Church against Itself.* New York: Herder and Herder, 1967.

Sanks, T. Howland. "Forms of Ecclesiality: The Analogical Church." *Theological Studies* 49 (1988): 695–708.

Schillebeeckx, Edward. *Church: The Human Story of God.* New York: Crossroad, 1990.

————. *God the Future of Man.* New York: Sheed & Ward, 1968.

————. *The Language of Faith: Essays on Jesus, Theology, and the Church.* Concilium Series. Maryknoll, N.Y.: Orbis, 1995.

————, ed. *L'avenir de l'Église.* Concilium, vol. 60, supplément. Paris: Mame, 1971.

Sesboüé, Bernard, ed. *Histoire des Dogmes.* Paris: Desclée. For ecclesiological themes see vol. 3, *Les signes du salut,* by H. Bourgeois, B. Sesboüé, and P. Tilon (1995), and vol. 4, *La parole du salut,* by Ch. Théobald and B. Sesboüé (1996).

Valentini, Donato, ed. *L'ecclesiologia contemporanea.* Padua: Messagero, 1994. Articles by T. Citrini, D. Valentini, S. Dianich, L. Sartori, and others.

Valeske, Ulrich. *Votum Ecclesiae,* pt. 2, 1–210. Munich: Claudius, 1962.

18

TWENTIETH-CENTURY
ORTHODOX ECCLESIOLOGY

Ecumenical questions are treated in section 24.

Afanassieff, Nicolas. *L'Église du Saint Esprit*. Paris: Cerf, 1975.

Allen, Joseph J. *The Ministry of the Church: Image of Pastoral Care*. Crestwood, N.Y.: St. Vladimir, 1986.

Barrois, Georges Augustin. *Jesus Christ and the Temple*. Crestwood, N.Y.: St. Vladimir, 1980.

Benz, Ernst. *The Eastern Orthodox Church*. Garden City, N.Y.: Doubleday Anchor Books, 1963.

Borelli, John, and John H. Erickson, eds. *The Quest for Unity: Orthodox and Catholics in Dialogue*. Crestwood, N.Y. and Washington, D.C.: St. Vladimir and USCC, 1996.

Bria, Ion. *The Sense of Ecumenical Tradition: The Ecumenical Witness and Vision of the Orthodox*. Geneva: World Council of Churches, 1991.

Bulgakov, Sergei Nikolayev. *L'épouse de l'agneau*. Lausanne: L'âge d'homme, 1984.

————. *Father Sergius Bulgakov–1871–1944: A Collection of Essays*. London: Fellowship of St. Alban and St. Sergius, 1969.

————. *The Orthodox Church*. New ed. Crestwood, N.Y.: St. Vladimir, 1988.

Clément, Olivier. *Dialogues avec le Patriarche Athénagoras*. Paris: Fayard, 1969.

Constantelos, Demetrios J. *Understanding the Greek Orthodox Church: Its Faith, History and Practice*. New York: Seabury, 1982.

Damaskinos, M., ed. *Église locale et Église Universelle*. Chambésy-Genève: Centre Orthodoxe du patriarcat oecuménique, 1981.

Erickson, John H. *The Challenge of Our Past: Studies in Orthodox Canon Law and Church History*. Crestwood, N.Y.: St. Vladimir, 1991.

Evdokimov, Paul. *L'Orthodoxie*, pp. 123–70. Neuchâtel: Delachaux & Niestlé, 1959.

Fahey, Michael A. *Orthodox and Catholic Sister Churches: East Is West and West Is East*. Milwaukee: Marquette University, 1996.

————. "Orthodox Ecumenism and Theology: 1978–83." *Theological Studies* 44 (1983): 625–92.

————. "Orthodox Ecumenism and Theology: 1970–78." *Theological Studies* 39 (1978): 446–85.

Florovsky, Georges. *Collected Works of Georges Florovsky*. 4 vols. Belmont, Mass.: Nordland, 1972–79.

————. *The Ecumenical World of Orthodox Civilization*. Edited by A. Blane. The Hague: Mouton, 1974.

Harakas, Stanley S. "The Local Church: An Eastern Orthodox Perspective." *Ecumenical Review* 29 (1977): 141–53.

Holtzmann, Jerome J. "Eucharistic Ecclesiology of the Orthodox Theologians." *Diakonia* 8 (1973): 5–21.

Khomiakov, Alexis S. "The Church is One." English translation in *Russia and the English Church During the Last Fifty Years*, edited by W. J. Birbeck, 1:193–223. London: Rivington, Percival, 1895. Republished, Westmead, Farnborough, Hants, England: Gregg International, 1969.

Lanne, Emmanuel. "Die Kirche als Mysterium und Institution in der Orthodoxen Theologie." In *Mysterium Kirche in der Sicht der theologische Disziplinen*, edited by F. Holböck and T. Sartory, 2:891–925. 2 vols. Salzburg: O. Muller, 1962.

Limouris, Gennadios, and Nomikos Michael Vapos, eds. *Orthodox Perspectives on Baptism, Eucharist, and Ministry*. Faith and Order Paper, no. 128. Brookline, Mass.: Holy Cross Orthodox Press; Geneva: World Council of Churches, 1985.

Luykx, Archimandrite Boniface. *Eastern Monasticism and the Future of the Church*. Stamford, Conn.: Basileos, 1993.

Meyendorff, John. *Byzantine Theology: Historical Trends and Doctrinal Themes*. New York: Fordham University, 1987.

*———. *Catholicity and the Church*. Crestwood, N.Y.: St. Vladimir, 1983.

———. *Living Tradition: Orthodox Witness in the Contemporary World*. Crestwood, N.Y.: St. Vladimir, 1978.

———. *The Orthodox Church*. New York: Pantheon Books, 1962.

Nichols, Aidan. *Rome and the Eastern Churches: A Study in Schism*. Collegeville, Minn.: Liturgical Press, 1992.

Nissiotis, Nikos A. "Pneumatological Christology as a Presupposition of Ecclesiology." In *Oecumenica: An Annual Symposium of Ecumenical Research 1967*, pp. 235–52. Minneapolis: Augsburg, 1967.

O'Leary, Paul P. *The Triune Church: A Study in the Ecclesiology of S. Xomjakov*. Dublin: Dominican Publications; Freiburg: Universitätsverlag, 1982.

Patelos, Constantine. *The Orthodox Church in the Ecumenical Move-ment: Documents and Statements 1902–1975*. Geneva: World Council of Churches, 1978.

Pomazansky, Michael. *Orthodox Dogmatic Theology: A Concise Expo-sition*. 2nd ed. Platina, Calif.: Saint Herman of Alaska Broth-erhood, 1994.

*Schmemann, Alexander. *Church, World, Mission: Reflections on Orthodoxy in the West*. Crestwood, N.Y.: St. Vladimir, 1979.

Staniloe, Dumitru. *Theology and the Church*. Crestwood, N.Y.: St. Vladimir, 1984.

Tomos Agapes: Vatican-Phanar (1958–1970). Rome: Polyglotte Vat-icane, 1971. Documentation of the dialogue between the Holy See and the Ecumenical Patriarch of Constantinople.

Tsirpanlis, Constantine N. *Introduction to Eastern Patristic Thought and Orthodox Theology*. Collegeville, Minn.: Liturgical Press, 1991.

Vries, Wilhelm de. *Orient et occident: Les structures ecclésiales vues dans l'histoire des sept premiers conciles oecuméniques*. Paris: Cerf, 1974.

*Ware, Timothy (Kallistos). *The Orthodox Church*. New ed. Lon-don and New York: Penguin, 1993.

*Zizioulas, J. D. *Being as Communion: Studies in Personhood and the Church*. Crestwood, N.Y.: St. Vladimir, 1985.

———. "The Pneumatological Dimension of the Church." *Com-munio* 1 (1974): 142–58.

19

TWENTIETH-CENTURY PROTESTANT AND ANGLICAN ECCLESIOLOGY

Ecumenical questions are treated in section 24.

Ackley, John B. *The Church of the Word: A Comparative Study of Word, Church, and Office in the Thought of Karl Rahner and Gerhard Ebeling.* New York: Peter Lang, 1993.

Alston, Wallace M., Jr. *Guides to the Reformed Tradition: The Church.* Atlanta: John Knox, 1984.

Aulén, Gustav, Anton Fridrichsen, et al. *Ein Buch von der Kirche.* Göttingen: Vandenhoeck & Ruprecht, 1951. Swedish scholars on biblical, historical, and systematic aspects of the church.

Avis, Paul. *Authority, Leadership, and Conflict in the Church.* Philadelphia: Trinity Press International, 1992.

Barth, Karl. *Church Dogmatics.* Vols. IV/1 and IV/2, *The Doctrine of Reconciliation.* Edinburgh: T & T Clark, 1956, 1958.

———. *Theology and Church: Shorter Writings 1920–1928.* London: SCM, 1962.

*Berkouwer, Gerrit C. *The Church*. Grand Rapids, Mich.: Wm. B. Eerdmans, 1976.

Bonhoeffer, Dietrich. *The Communion of Saints: A Dogmatic Inquiry into the Sociology of the Church*. New York: Harper & Row, 1963.

Brunner, Emil. *The Misunderstanding of the Church*. London: Lutterworth, 1952.

Ebeling, Gerhard. *Dogmatik des christlichen Glaubens*, vol. 3. Tübingen: J. C. B. Mohr, 1979.

Gilkey, Langdon. *How the Church Can Minister to the World without Losing Itself*. New York: Harper & Row, 1964.

*Gunton, Colin E., and Daniel W. Hardy, eds. *On Being the Church: Essays on the Christian Community*. Edinburgh: T & T Clark, 1989.

Haase, Wolfgang, ed. *Rome and the Anglicans: Historical and Doctrinal Aspects of Anglican–Roman Catholic Relations*. Berlin and New York: Walter de Gruyter, 1982.

Heinz, Gerhard. *Das Problem der Kirchenentstehung in der deutschen protestantischen Theologie des 20. Jahrhunderts*. Mainz: Matthias-Grünewald, 1974.

Hinson, E. Glenn. *The Integrity of the Church*. Nashville, Tenn.: Broadman, 1978.

Hodgson, Peter C. *Revisioning the Church: Ecclesial Freedom in the New Paradigm*. Philadelphia: Fortress, 1988.

Jenkins, Daniel. *The Strangeness of the Church*. Garden City, N.Y.: Doubleday, 1955.

Leith, John H. *The Church: A Believing Fellowship*. Atlanta: John Knox, 1981.

MacGregor, Geddes. *Corpus Christi: The Nature of the Church according to the Reformed Tradition.* Philadelphia: Westminster, 1958.

Marquart, Kurt E. *The Church and Her Fellowship, Ministry, and Governance.* Waverly, Ia.: International Foundation in Lutheran Confessional Research, 1990. This study presents the ecclesiology of the Lutheran Missouri Synod.

Minear, Paul. *Horizons of Christian Community.* St. Louis, Mo.: Bethany, 1959.

*Moltmann, Jürgen. *The Church in the Power of the Spirit.* New York: Harper and Row, 1977.

Mudge, Lewis S. *The Sense of a People: Toward a Church for the Human Future.* Philadelphia: Trinity Press International, 1992.

Nelson, J. Robert. *The Realm of Redemption: Studies in the Doctrine of the Nature of the Church in Contemporary Protestant Theology.* London: Epworth, 1951.

Newbigin, Lesslie. *The Household of God.* London: SCM, 1953.

Nygren, Anders. *Christ and His Church.* Philadelphia: Westminster, 1956.

Nygren, Anders, et al. *This Is the Church.* Philadelphia: Muhlenberg, 1962. Articles by Swedish Lutheran theologians: A. Nygren, G. Aulén, A. Fridrichsen, and others.

O'Grady, Colm. *The Church in the Theology of Karl Barth.* London: G. Chapman, 1968. Extensive bibliography.

—————. *The Church in Catholic Theology: Dialogue with Karl Barth.* London: G. Chapman, 1970.

Pannenberg, Wolfhart. *The Church.* Philadelphia: Westminster, 1983.

*————. *Systematic Theology*. Vol. 3. Grand Rapids, Mich.: Wm. B. Eerdmans, 1997. This volume presents his theology of church.

Runyon, Theodore, ed. *Hope for the Church: Moltmann in Dialogue with Practical Theology*. Nashville, Tenn.: Abingdon, 1979.

Schlink, Edmund. *The Coming Christ and the Coming Church*. Philadelphia: Fortress, 1968.

Sykes, Stephen, ed. *Authority in the Anglican Communion*. Toronto: Anglican Book Centre, 1987.

Tavard, George H. *A Review of Anglican Orders: The Problem and the Solution*. Collegeville, Minn.: Liturgical Press, 1990.

Visser't Hooft, Wilhelm A., and Joseph Oldham. *The Church and Its Function in Society*. Chicago: Willett, Clarke, 1927.

Volf, Miroslav. *After Our Likeness: The Church as the Image of the Trinity*. Grand Rapids, Mich.: Wm. B. Eerdmans, 1998.

*Welch, Claude. *The Reality of the Church*. New York: Scribner, 1958.

Williams, Colin W. *The Church*. Philadelphia: Westminster, 1958.

20

THE NATURE OF THE CHURCH

Only Roman Catholic authors are given here. Orthodox, Protestant, and Anglican works are given in their respective sections. See also section 17 for current trends in Roman Catholic ecclesiology.

Antón, Angel. *La Iglesia de Cristo*. Madrid: Biblioteca de autores cristianos, 1977.

*Auer, Johann. *The Church: The Universal Sacrament of Salvation*. Washington, D.C.: Catholic University of America, 1993.

Baril, Gilberte. *The Feminine Face of the People of God: Biblical Symbols of the Church as Bride and Mother*. Collegeville, Minn.: Liturgical Press, 1992.

Bouyer, Louis. *The Church of God: Body of Christ and Temple of the Holy Spirit*. Chicago: Franciscan Herald, 1982.

Bühlmann, Walbert. *The Church of the Future: A Model for the Year 2001*. Maryknoll, N.Y.: Orbis, 1986.

Butler, Basil Christopher. *The Idea of the Church*. Baltimore: Helicon, 1962.

Carmody, Denise Lardner, and John Tully Carmody. *Bonded in Christ's Love: An Introduction to Ecclesiology.* New York: Paulist, 1986.

Casel, Odo. *Mysterium der Ekklesia.* Mainz: Matthias-Grünewald, 1961.

Congar, Yves M.-J. *I Believe in the Holy Spirit.* 3 vols. New York: Seabury, 1983.

———. *The Mystery of the Church.* Baltimore: Helicon, 1960; 2nd ed., revised 1965.

———. *The Mystery of the Temple.* Westminster, Md.: Newman, 1962.

———. *Sainte Église: Études et approches ecclésiologiques.* Unam Sanctam, no. 41. Paris: Cerf, 1963. Articles published over thirty years.

Daniélou, Jean. *Le signe du temple.* Paris: Gallimard, 1942.

Dianich, Severino. *Chiesa in missione: Per una ecclesiologia dinamica.* Cinisello Balsamo: Paoline, 1987.

———. *La chiesa mistero di comunione.* Genoa: Marietti, 1987.

———. *Ecclesiologia: Questioni di methodo e una proposta.* Milan: Paoline, 1993.

Donovan, Daniel. *Distinctively Catholic: An Exploration of Catholic Identity.* New York and Mahwah, N.J.: Paulist, 1997.

Dóriga, Enrique L. *Jerauquía, infalibilidad y comunión intereclesial.* Barcelona: Herder, 1973.

*Dulles, Avery. *Models of the Church.* Garden City, N.Y.: Doubleday, 1974. Expanded ed., 1987.

Forte, Bruno. *La chiesa della Trinità: Saggio sul mistero della chiesa. Comunione e missione.* Milan: San Paolo, 1995.

———. *The Church: Icon of the Trinity.* Boston: Pauline, 1991.

Fries, Heinrich. *Aspects of the Church*. Westminster, Md.: Newman, 1966. A collection of essays on Catholic and ecumenical ecclesiology.

*————. *Fundamental Theology*. Washington, D.C.: Catholic University of America, 1996. Section on the church, 385–633.

Garijo-Guembe, Miguel M. *Communion of Saints: Foundation, Nature, and Structure of the Church*. Collegeville, Minn.: Liturgical Press, 1994.

International Theological Commission. "Selected Themes of Ecclesiology" in *ITC, Texts and Documents, 1969–1985*, edited by Michael Sharkey, 267–304. San Francisco: Ignatius, 1989.

Journet, Charles. *L'Église du Verbe Incarné*. 3 vols. Bruges: Desclée De Brouwer, 1941, 1951, 1969. Vol. 1 in English: *The Church of the Incarnate Word*. New York: Sheed & Ward, 1955.

Kehl, Medard. *Die Kirche: Eine Katholische Ekklesiologie*. Würzburg: Echter, 1992.

Kern, Walter, Hermann J. Pottmeyer, and Max Seckler, eds. *Handbuch der Fundamentaltheologie*. Vol. 3, *Traktat Kirche*. Freiburg, Basel, Vienna: Herder, 1986. Articles by V. Conzemius, H. Fries, M. Kehl, H. J. Pottmeyer, and others.

Kilian, Sabbas. "The Holy Spirit in Christ and in Christians." *American Benedictine Review* 20 (1969): 99–121.

*Küng, Hans. *The Church*. New York: Sheed & Ward, 1968. Paperback, New York: Doubleday Image, 1976. Criticisms and replies in *Diskussion um Hans Küng, 'Die Kirche,'* edited by H. Häring and J. Nolte. Freiburg: Herder, 1971.

Le Guillou, Marie-Joseph. *Christ and Church: A Theology of the Mystery*. New York: Desclée, 1966.

Lubac, Henri de. *Catholicism: A Study of Dogma in Relation to the Corporate Destiny of Mankind*. New York: Longmans, Green, 1950.

*————. *The Splendour of the Church*. New York: Sheed & Ward, 1956. Reprint, *The Splendor of the Church*. San Francisco: Ignatius, 1991.

Maritain, Jacques. *On the Church of Christ: The Person of the Church and Her Personnel*. Notre Dame, Ind.: University of Notre Dame, 1973.

McBrien, Richard. *Catholicism*, chaps. 16–26. San Francisco: Harper, 1994.

McNamara, Kevin. *Sacrament of Salvation*. Chicago: Franciscan Herald, 1981.

Mondin, G. Battista. *La chiesa: Primizia del regno. Trattato di ecclesiologia*. Bologna: Dehoniane, 1986.

Montcheuil, Yves de. *Aspects of the Church*. Chicago: Fides, 1955.

Mühlen, Heribert. *Una Mystica Persona*. 2nd ed. Paderborn: F. Schöningh, 1967. French version: *L'Esprit dans l'Église*. 2 vols. Paris: Cerf, 1969.

O'Grady, John F. *The Roman Catholic Church: Its Origin and Nature*. New York and Mahwah, N.J.: Paulist, 1997.

Powell, John. *The Mystery of the Church*. Milwaukee, Wis.: Bruce, 1967.

Salaverri, Ioachim. "De ecclesia Christi." In *Sacrae Theologiae Summa*, 4th ed., 1:501–993. Madrid: Biblioteca de autores cristianos, 1958.

Sanks, T. Howland. *Salt, Leaven, and Light: The Community Called Church*. New York: Crossroad, 1992.

Schmaus, Michael. *Dogma 4: The Church*. Kansas City, Mo.: Sheed & Ward, 1972.

————. *Katholische Dogmatik*. Vol. 3/1. Munich: M. Hueber, 1958.

Sullivan, Francis A. *De ecclesia*. Vol. 1, *Questiones theologiae fundamentalis*. Rome: Gregoriana, 1963. 2nd ed., 1965.

Tavard, George. *The Church, Community of Salvation: An Ecumenical Ecclesiology*. Collegeville, Minn.: Liturgical Press, 1992.

21

THE CHURCH AS BODY OF CHRIST AND PEOPLE OF GOD

Asmussen, Hans, et al. *Die Kirche Volk Gottes*. Stuttgart: Schwaben, 1961. Articles by Lutheran and Roman Catholic theologians: H. Asmussen, E. Hesse, W. Lehmann, and others.

Congar, Yves. "The Church: The People of God." In *The Church and Mankind,* edited by Edward Schillebeeckx, 11–37. Concilium, no. 1. Glen Rock, N.J.: Paulist, 1965.

Galot, Jean. *Dans le corps mystique*. Bruges: Desclée De Brouwer, 1961.

Keller, Max. *"Volk Gottes" als Kirchenbegriff: Eine Untersuchung zum neueren Verständnis*. Einsiedeln: Benziger, 1970.

Malmberg, Felix. *Ein Leib–ein Geist*. Freiburg: Herder, 1960.

*Mersch, Émile. *The Theology of the Mystical Body*. St. Louis, Mo.: B. Herder, 1958.

Mura, Ernest. *The Nature of the Mystical Body*. St. Louis, Mo.: B. Herder, 1963.

Norris, Frank B. *God's Own People: An Introductory Study of the Church*. Baltimore: Helicon, 1962.

Pelton, Robert S., ed. *The Church as the Body of Christ*. Notre Dame, Ind.: University of Notre Dame, 1963. Articles by W. J. Burghardt, B. Cooke, B. Ahern, K. E. Skydsgaard, and F. H. Littell.

Rahner, Karl. "People of God." In *Sacramentum Mundi*, 4:400–402. New York: Herder and Herder, 1968. Reprinted in *The Encyclopedia of Theology: The Concise Sacramentum Mundi*, pp. 1204-6. New York: Seabury, 1975.

Ratzinger, Joseph. *Das neue Volk Gottes: Entwürfe zur Ekklesiologie*. Düsseldorf: Patmos, 1969.

Robinson, John A. T. *The Body: A Study in Pauline Theology*. London: SCM, 1952.

Schnackenburg, Rudolf. "People of God." In *The Church in the New Testament*, 149-57. New York: Herder and Herder, 1965.

Schweizer, Eduard. *The Church as the Body of Christ*. Richmond, Va.: John Knox, 1964.

Tromp, Sebastian. *Corpus Christi quod est ecclesia*. 4 vols. Vol. 1, *Introductio generalis* (English translation: New York: Vantage, 1960); vol. 2, *De Christo capite mystici corporis;* vol. 3, *De Spiritu Christi anima;* vol. 4, *De virgine deipara Maria corde mystici corporis*. Rome: Gregoriana, 1946-72.

Vidal, Maurice. *L'Église, peuple de Dieu dans l'histoire des hommes*. Paris: Centurion, 1975.

22

THE CHURCH AS ONE, HOLY, CATHOLIC, AND APOSTOLIC

For holiness and unity of the church, see also sections 23 and 24 below.

Beinert, Wolfgang. *Um das dritte Kirchenattribut.* 2 vols. Essen: H. Wingen, 1964.

Brière, Yves de la. "Église (Question des Notes)." In *Dictionnaire apologétique de la foi catholique,* vol. 1, cols. 1268–1301. Paris: Beauchesne, 1925.

Catholicity and Apostolicity. Special issue of *One in Christ* 6/3 (1970). Report of the WCC-RC Joint Theological Commission, with articles by R. Schnackenburg, J. Bosc, J. Witte, W. Pannenberg, and others.

Congar, Yves M.-J. "Apostolicité de ministère et apostolicité de doctrine." In *Volk Gottes: Festgabe für J. Höfer,* edited by Remigius Bäumer and Heimo Dolch, 84–111. Freiburg: Herder, 1967.

———. "Catholicité." *Catholicisme,* 2:722–25. Paris: Letouzey, 1950.

———. L 'Église une, sainte, catholique, et apostolique. In *Mysterium Salutis,* no. 15. Paris: Cerf, 1970. German version: "Die Wesenseigenschaften der Kirche." In *Mysterium salutis,*

edited by Johannes Feiner and Magnus Löhrer, 4/1:357–599. Einsiedeln: Benziger, 1972.

———. *The Wide World My Parish: Salvation and Its Problems*. Baltimore: Helicon, 1961.

*Dulles, Avery. *The Catholicity of the Church*. Oxford: Clarendon, 1985.

Garciadiego, Alejandro. *Katholiké Ekklesia*. Mexico: Editorial Jus, 1953.

Hastings, Adrian. *One and Apostolic*. New York: Sheed & Ward, 1963.

Küng, Hans, ed. *Apostolic Succession: Rethinking a Barrier to Unity*. Concilium, no. 34. Glen Rock, N.J.: Paulist, 1968.

Lubac, Henri de. *Catholicism: A Study of Dogma in Relation to the Corporate Destiny of Mankind*. New York: Longmans, Green, 1950.

Neuner, Josef. "Die Weltkirche: Die Katholizität der Kirche in Missionswerk." In *Mysterium Kirche in der Sicht der theologische Disziplinen*, edited by F. Holböck and T. Sartory, 2:815–89. 2 vols. Salzburg: O. Müller, 1962.

Steinacker, Peter. *Die Kennzeichen der Kirche*. Berlin: Walter de Gruyter, 1982.

*Sullivan, Francis A. *The Church We Believe In: One, Holy, Catholic and Apostolic*. New York and Mahwah, N.J.: Paulist, 1988.

Thils, Gustave. *Les notes de l'Église dans l'apologétique catholique depuis la Réforme*. Gembloux: J. Duculot, 1937.

Witte, Jan L. "L'Église, Sacramentum Unitatis du cosmos et du genre humain." In *L'Église de Vatican II*, edited by G. Baraúna, 2:457–91. Unam Sanctam, no. 51b. Paris: Cerf, 1966. Italian version: *La Chiesa del Vaticano II*. Florence: Vallecchi, 1965. German version: *De Ecclesia: Beiträge zur Konsti-*

tution über die Kirche des II. Vatikanischen Konzils. Freiburg: Herder, 1966.

———. "One, Holy, Catholic, and Apostolic." In *One, Holy, Catholic, and Apostolic*, edited by Herbert Vorgrimler, 1–43. London: Sheed & Ward, 1968.

23

THE HOLINESS OF THE CHURCH

Balthasar, Hans Urs von. "Casta Meretrix." In *Spouse of the Word: Explorations in Theology*, 2:193–288. San Francisco: Ignatius, 1991.

Biffi, Giacomo. *"Casta Meretrix": Saggio sull'ecclesiologia di San Ambrogio*. Casale Monferrato: Piemme, 1996.

Congar, Yves M.-J. "L'Église est sainte." *Angelicum* 42 (1965): 273–98.

Cottier, Georges. "Église sainte: L'Église sans péché non sans pécheurs." *Nova et vetera* 66 (1991): 9-27.

Doignon, J. *"Peccatrix ecclesia*: Une formule d'inspiration origenienne chez Hilaire de Poitiers." *Revue des sciences philsophiques et théologiques* 74 (1990): 255–58.

Laszlo, Stephen. "Sin in the Holy Church of God." In *Council Speeches of Vatican II*, edited by Hans Küng et al., 44–48. Glen Rock, N.J.: Paulist Deus Books, 1964.

*Latourelle, René. *Christ and the Church: Signs of Salvation*, 211–64. Staten Island, N.Y.: Alba House, 1972.

Molinari, Paolo. *Saints: Their Place in the Church*. New York: Sheed & Ward, 1965.

O'Callaghan, Paul. "The Holiness of the Church in *Lumen Gentium*." *Thomist* 52 (1988): 673–701.

Rahner, Karl. "The Church of Sinners." In *Theological Investigations*, 6:253–69. New York: Crossroad, 1969.

———. "The Church of the Saints." In *Theological Investigations*, 3:91–104. New York: Crossroad, 1967.

*———. "The Sinful Church in the Decrees of Vatican II." In *Theological Investigations*, 6:270–94. New York: Crossroad, 1967.

Smith, Robert D. *The Mark of Holiness*. Westminster, Md.: Newman, 1961.

Stöhr, Johannes. "Heilige Kirche-Sündige Kirche?" *Münchener theologische Zeitschrift* 18 (1967): 119–42.

24

THE UNITY OF THE CHURCH

The following are helpful sources for the study of ecumenism, especially in the area of ecclesiology. Studies of the Ecumenical Movement are too numerous to be listed here.

Six collections of ecumenical documents have been published.

Burgess, Joseph A., and Jeffrey Gros, eds. *Building Unity: Ecumenical Dialogues with Roman Catholic Participation in the United States.* Ecumenical Documents IV. New York and Mahwah, N.J.: Paulist, 1989.

———. *Growing Consensus: Church Dialogues in the United States, 1962–1991.* Ecumenical Documents V. New York and Mahwah, N.J.: Paulist, 1995.

Meyer, Harding, and Lukas Vischer, eds. *Growth in Agreement: Reports and Agreed Statements of Ecumenical Conversations on a World Level.* Ecumenical Documents II. New York: Paulist; Geneva: World Council of Churches, 1984.

Rusch, William G., and Jeffrey Gros, eds. *Deepening Communion: International Ecumenical Documents with Roman Catholic Participation.* Washington, D.C.: United States Catholic Conference, 1988.

Stormon, E. J., ed. *Towards the Healing of Schism: The Sees of Rome and Constantinople. Public Statements and Correspondence*

Between the Holy See and the Ecumenical Patriarchate 1958–1984. Ecumenical Documents III. New York and Mahwah, N.J.: Paulist, 1987.

Stransky, Thomas F., and John B. Sheerin, eds. *Doing the Truth in Charity: Statements of Pope Paul VI, Popes John Paul I and John Paul II, and the Secretariat for Promoting Christian Unity 1964–1980.* Ecumenical Documents I. New York: Paulist, 1982.

• • •

Backman, Milton V., Jr. *Christian Churches of America: Origins and Beliefs.* New York: Scribner, 1976.

Bria, Ion, and Dagmar Heller, eds. *Ecumenical Pilgrims: Profiles of Pioneers in Christian Reconciliation.* Geneva: World Council of Churches, 1995.

Bulletin of the Centro Pro Unione (Rome). "A Bibliography of Interchurch and Interconfessional Theological Dialogues." Published annually by the Centro Pro Unione, Via Maria dell'Anima, 30; 00186 Rome, Italy.

Dictionary of Christianity in America. Downers Grove, Ill.: Intervarsity, 1990.

Eldern, Marlin van. *Introducing the World Council of Churches.* Geneva: World Council of Churches, 1990.

Fahey, Michael A. *Ecumenism: A Bibliographical Overview.* Westport, Conn.: Greenwood, 1992.

Fey, Harold E., ed. *The Ecumenical Advance: A History of the Ecumenical Movement, 1948–1968.* London: SPCK, 1970. New ed., Geneva: WCC Publications, 1986.

Lossky, Nicholas, et al., eds. *Dictionary of the Ecumenical Movement.* Geneva: World Council of Churches; Grand Rapids, Mich.: Wm. B. Eerdmans, 1991. In addition to the individual articles, the bibliographical references are most useful.

Melton, J. Gordon. *Religious Bodies in the United States: A Directory*. New York: Garland, 1992.

Pontifical Council for Promoting Christian Unity. "Directory for the Application of Principles and Norms of Ecumenism." *Origins* (July 29, 1993): 129, 131–60.

Roberson, Ronald G. *The Eastern Christian Churches: A Brief Survey*. Rome, Orientalia Christiana, 1995.

Rouse, Ruth, and Stephen Charles Neill, eds. *A History of the Ecumenical Movement 1517–1948*. Philadelphia: Westminster, 1968. New ed., Geneva: WCC Publications, 1986.

Shriver, Peggy L. *Having Gifts that Differ: Profiles of Ecumenical Churches*. New York: Friendship, 1989.

World Council of Churches. *Baptism, Eucharist and Ministry*. Faith and Order Paper no. 111. Geneva: World Council of Churches, 1982.

World Council of Churches. *Handbook of Member Churches*. Geneva: World Council of Churches, 1982.

• • •

Baum, Gregory. "The Ecclesial Reality of Other Churches." In *The Church and Ecumenism*, edited by Hans Küng, 62–86. Concilium, no. 4. Glen Rock, N.J.: Paulist, 1965.

————. *Progress and Perspectives*. New York: Sheed & Ward, 1962. Paperback: *The Catholic Quest for Christian Unity*. Glen Rock, N.J.: Paulist Deus Books, 1965.

————. *That They May Be One: A Study of Papal Doctrine*. Westminster, Md.: Newman, 1958.

Bea, Augustin. *Ecumenism in Focus*. London: Geoffrey Chapman, 1969.

————. *The Unity of Christians*. New York: Herder and Herder, 1963.

————. *The Way to Unity after the Council*. New York: Herder and Herder, 1967.

Bea, Augustin, and Willem A. Visser't Hooft. *Peace among Christians*. New York: Association and Herder and Herder, 1970.

*Becker, Werner, and Johannes Feiner. "Decree on Ecumenism." In *Commentary on the Documents of Vatican II*, edited by Herbert Vorgrimler, 2:1–164. New York: Herder and Herder, 1968.

Bermejo, Luis M. *Towards Christian Unity*. Lanham, Md.: University Press of America, 1987.

Braaten, Carl E. *Mother Church: Ecclesiology and Ecumenism*. Minneapolis: Fortress, 1998.

Brown, Robert McAfee. *The Ecumenical Revolution*. Rev. ed. Garden City, N.Y.: Doubleday Image Books, 1969.

Burgess, Joseph A., ed. *In Search of Christian Unity: Basic Consensus/Basic Differences*. Minneapolis: Fortress, 1991.

Butler, Basil Christopher. *The Church and Unity: An Essay*. London: Geoffrey Chapman, 1979.

*Congar, Yves M.-J. *Dialogue Between Christians*. Westminster, Md.: Newman, 1966. A collection of previously published articles with a new introduction.

————. *Diversity and Communion*. Mystic, Conn.: Twenty-Third, 1985.

————. *Divided Christendom: A Catholic Study of the Problem of Reunion*. London: G. Bles, 1939.

————. *Ecumenism and the Future of the Church*. Chicago: Priory, 1967.

Cullmann, Oscar. *Unity through Diversity and A Contribution to the Discussion Concerning the Possibilities of its Actualization*. Philadelphia: Fortress, 1988.

————. *Vrai et faux oecuménisme: Oecuménisme après le concile.* Paris: Delachaux et Niestlé, 1971.

Dick, John A. *The Malines Conversations Revisited.* Leuven: Leuven University, 1989.

Dulles, Avery. "The Church, the Churches, and the Catholic Church." *Theological Studies* 33 (1972): 199–234.

————. "Method in Ecumenical Theology." In *The Craft of Theology: From Symbol to System*, 179–95. New York: Crossroad, 1992.

Duquoc, Christian. *Provisional Churches: An Essay in Ecumenical Ecclesiology.* London: SCM, 1986.

*Evans, Gillian R. *The Church and the Churches: Towards an Ecumenical Ecclesiology.* Cambridge and New York: Cambridge University, 1994.

————. *Method in Ecumenical Theology: The Lessons So Far.* Cambridge and New York: Cambridge University, 1996.

Fahey, Michael A., ed. *Catholic Perspectives on Baptism, Eucharist, and Ministry.* Lanham, Md.: University Press of America, 1986.

Flew, Robert Newton, ed. *The Nature of the Church.* Papers presented to the Third World Conference on Faith and Order. New York: Harper, 1952.

Ford, John T., and Darlis J. Swan, eds. *Twelve Tales Untold: A Study Guide for Ecumenical Reception.* Grand Rapids, Mich.: Wm. B. Eerdmans, 1993.

Fries, Heinrich, and Karl Rahner. *Unity of the Churches: An Actual Possibility.* Philadelphia: Fortress; New York: Paulist, 1985.

Gros, Jeffrey, Eamon McManus, and Ann Riggs. *Introduction to Ecumenism.* New York and Mahwah, N.J.: Paulist, 1998.

Groupe des Dombes. *For the Conversion of the Churches*. Geneva: World Council of Churches, 1993.

———. *Pour la communion des Eglises*. Paris: Centurion, 1988.

*John Paul II. Encyclical *Ut Unum Sint*. *Origins* 25 (June 8, 1995): 49, 51–72.

Kinnamon, Michael, and Brian E. Cope, eds. *The Ecumenical Movement: An Anthology of Key Texts and Voices*. Grand Rapids, Mich.: Wm. B. Eerdmans, 1997.

Lambert, Bernard. *Ecumenism: Theology and History*. New York: Herder and Herder, 1967.

Leeming, Bernard. *The Churches and the Church: A Study of Ecumenism with a New Postscript*. Westminster, Md.: Newman, 1963.

———. *The Vatican Council and Christian Unity*. New York: Harper & Row, 1966.

Le Guillou, Marie-Joseph. *Mission et unité: exigences de la communion*. Unam Sanctam, nos. 33–34. Paris: Cerf, 1960.

Lutheran–Roman Catholic Joint Commission. *Church and Justification: Understanding the Church in the Light of the Doctrine of Justification*. Geneva: Lutheran World Federation, 1994.

McDonnell, Kilian. "The Concept of 'Church' in the Documents of Vatican II as Applied to Protestant Denominations." *Worship* 44 (1970): 332–49. Also found in Paul C. Empie and T. Austin Murphy, eds. *Eucharist and Ministry*. Lutherans and Catholics in Dialogue, vol. 4, 307–24. Minneapolis: Augsburg, 1979.

McGovern, James O. *The Church in the Churches*. Washington, D.C.: Corpus, 1968.

Minus, Paul. *The Catholic Rediscovery of Protestantism: A History of Roman Catholic Ecumenical Pioneering*. New York: Paulist, 1976.

Mudge, Lewis S. *The Church as Moral Community: Ecclesiology and Ethics in Ecumenical Debate*. New York: Continuum, 1997.

Mühlen, Heribert. "Der eine Geist Christi und die vielen Kirchen." In *Una Mystica Persona*, 494–567. 2nd ed. Paderborn: F. Schöningh, 1967. French version: "L'unique Esprit du Christ et les multiples Églises." In *L'Esprit dans l'Église*, 2:175–263. Paris: Cerf, 1969.

Nilson, Jon. *Nothing Beyond the Necessary: Roman Catholicism and the Ecumenical Future*. New York and Mahwah, N.J.: Paulist, 1995.

Norgren, William. *Ecumenism of the Possible: Witness, Theology, and the Future Church*. Cincinnati, Oh.: Forward Movement, 1991.

O'Gara, Margaret. *The Ecumenical Gift Exchange*. Collegeville, Minn.: Liturgical Press, 1998.

Raiser, Konrad. *Ecumenism in Transition: A Paradigm Shift in the Ecumenical Movement?* Geneva: World Council of Churches, 1991.

Ratzinger, Joseph. *Church, Ecumenism, and Politics*. New York: Crossroad, 1988.

Ruggieri, Giuseppe, and Miklos Tomka, eds. *The Church in Fragments: Toward What Kind of Unity?* Concilium 1997/3. London: SCM; Maryknoll, N.Y.: Orbis, 1997. Articles by J.-P. Jossua, G. Baum, D. Tracy, and others.

Rusch, William G. *A Movement Toward Church Unity*. Philadelphia: Fortress, 1985.

———. *Reception: An Ecumenical Opportunity*. Philadelphia: Fortress, 1987.

Schlink, Edmund. *The Coming Christ and the Coming Church*. Philadelphia: Fortress, 1968.

*Thils, Gustave. *L'Église et les Églises: Perspectives nouvelles*. Bruges: Desclée De Brouwer, 1967.

Thurian, Max, ed. *Ecumenical Perspectives on Baptism, Eucharist and Ministry*. Geneva: World Council of Churches, 1983. Articles by L. Vischer, E. Lanne, G. Wainwright, A. Houtepen, and others.

Vanderwilt, Jeffrey. *A Church Without Borders: The Eucharist and the Church in Ecumenical Perspective*. Collegeville, Minn.: Liturgical Press, 1998.

Wainwright, Geoffrey. *The Ecumenical Moment: Crisis and Opportunity for the Church*. Grand Rapids, Mich.: Wm. B. Eerdmans, 1983.

World Council of Churches. *Man's Disorder and God's Design*. Vol. 1, *The Universal Church in God's Design*. New York: Harper & Bros. 1949. Papers prepared for the First Assembly of the World Council of Churches, Amsterdam, Holland.

Yarnold, Edward. *In Search of Unity*. Collegeville, Minn.: Liturgical Press, 1990.

25

MEMBERSHIP IN THE CHURCH

Carrier, Hervé. *The Sociology of Religious Belonging*. New York: Herder and Herder, 1965.

Dejaifve, Georges. "L'appartenance à l'Église du Concile de Florence à Vatican II." *Nouvelle revue théologique* 99 (1977): 21–50.

*Dulles, Avery. *Church Membership as a Catholic and Ecumenical Problem*. Milwaukee, Wis.: Marquette University, 1974, 1981.

Hughes, M. "The Juridical Nature of Joining the Catholic Church." *Studia Canonica* 8 (1974): 45–74, 379–431.

Internationale katholische Zeitschrift Communio, 5/3 (1976). Theme issue on church membership with articles by K. Lehmann, Y. M.-J. Congar, J. Ratzinger, and H. Urs von Balthasar.

Manson, T. W. "Entry into Membership of the Early Church." *Journal of Theological Studies* 48 (1947): 25–33.

Menges, Walter, and Norbert Greinacher. *Die Zugehörigkeit zur Kirche*. Mainz: Matthias-Grünewald, 1964.

———. "Members of the Church: *Mystici Corporis* and St. Thomas." *American Ecclesiastical Review* 148 (1963): 113–28, 167–84.

O'Neill, Colman E. "St. Thomas on the Membership of the Church." *Thomist* 27 (1963): 88–140.

Rahner, Karl. "Kirchengliedschaft. II. Dogmatisch." In *Lexikon für Theologie und Kirche*, vol. 61, cols. 223–25. Freiburg: Herder, 1961.

————. "Membership of the Church According to the Teaching of Pius XII's Encyclical, '*Mystici Corporis Christi.*'" In *Theological Investigations*, 2:1–88. New York: Crossroad, 1963.

Sauras, Emilio. "Church. 5. Membership of the Church." In *Sacramentum Mundi*, 1:332–37. New York: Herder and Herder, 1968. Bibliography.

————. "The Members of the Church." *Thomist* 27 (1963): 78–87.

Willems, Boniface. "Who Belongs to the Church?" In *The Church and Mankind*, edited by Edward Schillebeeckx, 131–51. Concilium, no. 1. Glen Rock, N.J.: Paulist, 1965. Survey of literature.

26

THE CHURCH AND SALVATION: THE NECESSITY OF THE CHURCH

Burghardt, Walter J., and William G. Thompson, eds. *Why the Church?* New York: Paulist, 1977. Reprint from *Theological Studies* 37/4 (1976). Articles by J. P. Schineller; E. A. LaVerdiere, and W. G. Thompson; J. P. Burns; R. D. Haight, and R. T. Sears.

Congar, Yves M.-J. "No Salvation Outside the Church?" In *The Wide World My Parish: Salvation and Its Problems*. Baltimore: Helicon, 1961.

Conway, Eamonn. *The Anonymous Christian–A Relativised Christianity? An Evaluation of Hans Urs von Balthasar's Criticism of Karl Rahner's Theory of the Anonymous Christian*. Frankfurt: Peter Lang, 1993.

Eminyan, Maurice. *The Theology of Salvation*. Boston: Daughters of St. Paul, 1960.

Fenton, Joseph C. *The Catholic Church and Salvation in the Light of Recent Pronouncements by the Holy See*. Westminster, Md.: Newman, 1958.

International Theological Commission. "Christianity and the World Religions." *Origins* (Aug. 14, 1997): 149, 151–66.

Kern, Walter. *Ausserhalb der Kirche kein Heil?* Freiburg: Herder, 1979.

King, John J. *The Necessity of the Church for Salvation in Selected Writings of the Past Century*. Washington, D.C.: Catholic University of America, 1960.

Lombardi, Riccardo. *The Salvation of the Unbeliever*. Westminster, Md.: Newman, 1960.

Rahner, Karl. *Theological Investigations*, vols. 1, 5, 6, 12, 14, and 16. New York: Crossroad. Articles on the salvation of non-Christians and anonymous Christianity.

Röper, Anita. *The Anonymous Christian*. New York: Sheed & Ward, 1966.

Schlette, Heinz Robert. *Towards a Theology of Religions*. New York: Herder and Herder, 1966.

*Sullivan, Francis A. *Salvation Outside the Church? Tracing the History of the Catholic Response*. New York and Mahwah, N.J.: Paulist, 1992.

Theisen, Jerome P. *The Ultimate Church and the Promise of Salvation*. Collegeville, Minn.: St. John's University, 1976.

27

EVANGELIZATION AND MISSIONARY ACTIVITY

See also sections 49, 50, 51.

Anderson, Gerald H., *Bibliography of the Theology of Missions in the Twentieth Century*. 3rd ed., revised and enlarged. New York: Missionary Research Library, 1966.

————, ed. *The Theology of Christian Mission*. New York: McGraw-Hill, 1961. Paperback ed., 1965.

Anderson, Gerald H., and Thomas F. Stransky, eds. *Mission Trends*. Nos. 1ff. New York: Paulist, 1974–.

Blauw, Johannes. *The Missionary Nature of the Church*. New York and London: McGraw-Hill, 1962.

Bohr, David. *Evangelization in America*. New York: Paulist, 1977.

*Bosch, David J. *Transforming Mission: Paradigm Shifts in Theology of Mission*. Maryknoll, N.Y.: Orbis, 1991.

Braaten, Carl E. *The Apostolic Imperative: Nature and Aim of the Church's Mission and Ministry*. Minneapolis: Augsburg, 1985.

————. *The Flaming Center: A Theology of Christian Mission*. Philadelphia: Fortress, 1977.

Brechter, Suso. "Decree on the Church's Missionary Activity." In *Commentary on the Documents of Vatican II*, edited by Herbert Vorgrimler, 4:87–181. New York: Herder and Herder, 1969.

*Bühlmann, Walbert. *The Coming of the Third Church*. Maryknoll, N.Y.: Orbis, 1977.

———. *Courage Church*. Maryknoll, N.Y.: Orbis, 1978.

———. *God's Chosen Peoples*. Maryknoll, N.Y.: Orbis, 1982.

———. *The Missions on Trial*. Maryknoll, N.Y.: Orbis, 1979.

*Burrows, William R. *Redemption and Dialogue: Reading* Redemptoris Missio *and* Dialogue and Proclamation. Maryknoll, N.Y.: Orbis, 1993.

Comblin, Joseph. *The Meaning of Mission: Jesus, Christians, and the Wayfaring Church*. Maryknoll, N.Y.: Orbis, 1977.

Costas, Orlando E. *The Integrity of Mission: The Inner Life and Outreach of the Church*. San Francisco: Harper & Row, 1979.

Cote, Richard G. *Re-Visioning Mission: The Catholic Church and Culture in Postmodern America*. New York and Mahwah, N.J.: Paulist, 1996.

Cotter, James P., ed. *The Word in the Third World*. Washington, D.C.: Corpus, 1968.

Davies, John G. *Worship and Mission*. New York: Association, 1967.

Dhavamony, Mariasusai, ed. *Prospettive di missiologia oggi*. Rome: Gregoriana, 1982.

Donovan, Vincent J. *Christianity Rediscovered*. Maryknoll, N.Y.: Orbis, 1978.

*Flanagan, Padraig, ed. *A New Missionary Era*. Maryknoll, N.Y.: Orbis, 1982. Articles by E. McDonagh, J. Comblin, B. Hearne, W. Bühlmann, and others.

Giordano, Pasquale B. *Awakening to Mission: The Philippine Church 1965-1981*. Quezon City, Philippines: New Day, 1988.

Glasser, Arthur F., and Donald A. McGavran. *Contemporary Theologies of Mission*. Grand Rapids, Mich.: Baker, 1983.

Greinacher, Norbert, and Alois Müller, eds. *Evangelization in the World Today*. Concilium, no. 114. New York: Seabury, 1979.

Hahn, Ferdinand. *Mission in the New Testament*. Studies in Biblical Literature, no. 47. Naperville, Ill.: Allenson, 1958.

Hale, J. Russell. *The Unchurched: Who They Are and Why They Stay Away*. New York: Harper & Row, 1980.

Hastings, Adrian. *Church and Mission in Modern Africa*. London: Burns & Oates, 1967. Reprint, New York: Fordham University, 1980.

Hillman, Eugene. *The Church as Mission*. New York: Herder and Herder, 1965.

————. *The Wider Ecumenism*. London: Burns & Oates, 1968.

Hocking, William E., ed. *Re-Thinking Missions: A Layman's Inquiry after 100 Years*. New York: Harper, 1932.

Hoekendijk, Johannes C. *The Church Inside Out*. Philadelphia: Westminster, 1966.

Hoffman, Ronan. *Pioneer Theories of Mission*. Washington, D.C.: Catholic University of America, 1960.

Illich, Ivan. *The Church, Change, and Development*. Chicago: Urban Training Center, 1970.

Istituto Paolo VI. *L'esortazione apostolica "Evangelii Nuntiandi." Storia, contenuti, ricezione*. Brescia: Istituto Paolo VI, 1998.

Jenkinson, William, and Helene O'Sullivan, eds. *Trends in Mis-*

sion: Toward the 3rd Millennium. Maryknoll, N.Y.: Orbis, 1991.

*John Paul II. *On the Permanent Validity of the Church's Missionary Mandate.* Encyclical *Redemptoris Missio. Origins* 20 (Jan. 31, 1991): 541–68.

The Jurist 39/1–2 (1979). Entire issue devoted to "The Church as Mission." Articles by J. H. Provost, R. D. Haight, D. Bohr, C. F. Jegen, J. A. Coleman, and others.

Kroeger, James H. *Living Mission: Challenges in Evangelization Today.* Maryknoll, N.Y.: Orbis, 1994.

LaVerdiere, Eugene, ed. *A Church for All Peoples: Missionary Issues in a World Church.* Collegeville, Minn.: Liturgical Press, 1993. Articles by A. Dulles, F. E. George, J.A. DiNoia, and others.

Luzbetak, Louis. *The Church and Cultures: New Perspectives in Missiological Anthropology.* Maryknoll, N.Y.: Orbis, 1988.

Martin, Ralph, and Peter Williamson, eds. *John Paul II and the New Evangelization.* San Francisco: Ignatius, 1995.

McDonagh, Enda, ed. *The Church is Mission.* Cleveland: World, 1969.

Motte, Mary, and Joseph R. Lang, eds. *Mission in Dialogue.* The SEDOS Research Seminar on the Future of Mission. Maryknoll, N.Y.: Orbis, 1982.

*Paul VI. *On Evangelization in the Modern World* (Apostolic Exhortation *Evangelii Nuntiandi*). Washington, D.C.: USCC, 1976.

Power, John. *Mission Theology Today.* Maryknoll, N.Y.: Orbis, 1971.

Rahner, Karl. "Grundprinzipien zur heutigen Mission der Kirche." In *Handbuch der Pastoraltheologie,* edited by F. X. Arnold et al., 2:46–80. Freiburg: Herder, 1966.

————, ed. *Rethinking the Church's Mission.* Concilium, no. 13. Glen Rock, N.J.: Paulist, 1966.

Roozen, David A. *The Churched and the Unchurched in America.* Washington, D.C.: Glenmary Research Center, 1978.

Scherer, James A. *Gospel, Church, and Kingdom: Comparative Studies in World Mission Theology.* Minneapolis: Augsburg, 1987.

Scherer, James A., and Stephen B. Bevans, eds. *New Directions in Mission and Evangelization.* No. 1, *Basic Statements 1974–1991.* Maryknoll, N.Y.: Orbis, 1992. No. 2, *Theological Foundations.* Maryknoll, N.Y.: Orbis, 1994.

Senior, Donald, and Carroll Stuhlmueller. *The Biblical Foundations for Mission.* Maryknoll, N.Y.: Orbis, 1983.

Seumois, André. *Théologie missionnaire.* 5 vols. Rome: Urbaniana, 1973–81.

Shorter, Aylward. *The Theology of Mission.* Notre Dame, Ind.: Fides, 1972.

Sweazey, George E. *The Church as Evangelist.* San Francisco and London: Harper & Row, 1984.

Verstraelen, F. J., A. Camps, L. A. Hodemaker, and M. R. Spindler, eds. *Missiology: An Ecumenical Introduction. Texts and Contexts of Global Christianity.* Grand Rapids, Mich.: Wm. B. Eerdmans, 1995.

Walls, Andrew F. *The Missionary Movement in Christian History.* Maryknoll, N.Y.: Orbis, 1996.

28

THE CHURCH AND SACRAMENTALITY

Boff, Leonardo. *Die Kirche als Sakrament im Horizont der Welter-fahrung.* Paderborn: F. Schöningh, 1972.

Congar, Yves M.-J. "L''Ecclesia' ou communauté chrétienne, sujet intégral de l'action liturgique." In *La liturgie après Vatican II,* edited by Yves Congar and Jean-Pierre Jossua, 241–82. Unam Sanctam, no. 66. Paris: Cerf, 1967.

———. *Un peuple messianique: L'Église sacrament du salut, salut et liberation.* Paris: Cerf, 1975.

Dulles, Avery. "The Church: Sacrament and Ground of Faith." In *Problems and Perspectives of Fundamental Theology,* edited by René Latourelle and Gerald O'Collins, 259–73. New York: Paulist, 1982.

Elert, Werner. *Eucharist and Church Fellowship in the First Four Centuries.* St. Louis, Mo.: Concordia, 1966.

Forte, Bruno. *La chiesa nell'Eucharistia: Per un'ecclesiologia eucharistica alla luce del Vaticano II.* Naples: D'Auria, 1975.

Häring, Bernard. *Sacraments and Your Everyday Life.* Liguori, Mo.: Liguori, 1976.

Kasper, Walter. "Die Kirche als universales Sakrament des Heils." In *Glaube im Prozess: Christsein nach dem II. Vatikanum. Für Karl Rahner,* edited by Elmar Klinger and Klaus Wittstadt, 221–39. Freiburg: Herder, 1984.

*Latourelle, René. *Christ and the Church: Signs of Salvation.* Staten Island, N.Y.: Alba House, 1972.

Lubac, Henri de. *Corpus Mysticum: L'eucharistie et l'Église au moyen âge.* Paris: Aubier, 1944.

*McPartlan, Paul. *The Eucharist Makes the Church: Henri de Lubac and John Zizioulas in Dialogue.* Edinburgh: T & T Clark, 1993.

———. *Sacrament of Salvation: An Introduction to Eucharistic Ecclesiology.* Edinburgh: T & T Clark, 1995.

Murphy-O'Connor, Jerome. "Eucharist and Community in First Corinthians." *Worship* 50 (1976): 370–85; 51 (1977): 56–69.

Navarro Lisbona, Antonio. *La Iglesia sacramento de Cristo sacerdote.* Salamanca: Sígueme, 1965.

Przewozny, Bernard. *Church as the Sacrament of the Unity of All Mankind in "Lumen Gentium" and "Gaudium et Spes" and in Semmelroth, Schillebeeckx, and Rahner.* Rome: Miscellanea Francescana, 1979.

*Rahner, Karl. *The Church and the Sacraments.* New York: Crossroad, 1963.

Rauch, Albert, and Paul Imhof, eds. *Die Eucharistie der einen Kirche: Eucharistische Ekklesiologie–Perspektiven und Grenzen.* Munich: Gerhard Kaffke, 1983.

*Schillebeeckx, Edward. *Christ the Sacrament of the Encounter with God.* New York: Sheed & Ward, 1963.

Semmelroth, Otto. *Church and Sacrament.* Notre Dame, Ind.: Fides, 1965.

————. *Die Kirche als Ursakrament*. Frankfurt: J. Knecht, 1953. French translation: *L'Église sacrement de la rédemption*. Paris: S. Paul, 1963.

Smulders, Peter. "L'Église sacrement du salut." In *L'Église de Vatican II*, edited by G. Baraúna, 2:313–38. Unam Sanctam, no. 51b. Paris: Cerf, 1966. Italian version: *La Chiesa del Vaticano II*. Florence: Vallecchi, 1965. German version: *De Ecclesia: Beiträge zur Konstitution über die Kirche des II. Vatikanischen Konzils*. Freiburg: Herder, 1966.

Thaler, Anton. *Gemeinde und Eucharistie: Grundlegung einer eucharistischen Ekklesiologie*. Freiburg (Switzerland): Universitätsverlag, 1988.

29

THE CHURCH AS COMMUNION

Acerbi, Antonio. *Due ecclesiologie: Ecclesiologia giuridica ed ecclesiologia di comunione nella "Lumen gentium."* Bologna: Dehoniane, 1975.

Avis, Paul. *Christians in Communion.* Collegeville, Minn.: Liturgical Press, 1990.

Benko, Stephen. *The Meaning of Sanctorum Communio.* Naperville, Ill.: A. R. Allenson, 1964.

*Congregation for the Doctrine of the Faith. "Some Aspects of the Church Understood as Communion" (*Communionis notio*). *Origins* 20 (June 25, 1992): 108–12. See also an unsigned article on the first anniversary of *Communionis notio* in *L'Osservatore Romano* (English edition), 4 July, 1993, pp. 4 and 10.

———. "The Church as Communion." In *New Perspectives in Historical Theology: Essays in Memory of John Meyendorff,* edited by Bradley Nassif, 125–39. Grand Rapids, Mich.: Wm. B. Eerdmans, 1996.

Dulles, Avery. "Communion." In *Dictionary of the Ecumenical Movement,* 206–9. Geneva: World Council of Churches and Grand Rapids, Mich.: Wm. B. Eerdmans, 1991.

Franco, E. *Comunione e partecipazione: La koinonia nell'epistolario Paolino*. Brescia: Morcelliana, 1986.

Galvin, John P. "The Church as Communion: Comments on a Letter of the Congregation for the Doctrine of the Faith." *One in Christ* 29 (1993): 310–17.

Garijo-Guembe, Miguel M. *Communion of Saints: Foundation, Nature, and Structure of the Church*. Collegeville, Minn.: Liturgical Press, 1994.

Granfield, Patrick, ed. *The Church and Communication*. Kansas City, Mo.: Sheed & Ward, 1994. Articles by P. Granfield, K. Kienzler, H. J. Pottmeyer, F. A. Sullivan, and others.

Hamer, Jerome. *The Church is a Communion*. New York: Sheed & Ward, 1964.

Hertling, Ludwig. *Communio: Church and Papacy in Early Christianity*. Introduction by Jared Wicks. Chicago: Loyola University, 1972.

Holze, Heinrich, ed. *The Church as Communion: Lutheran Contributions to Ecclesiology*. Geneva: Lutheran World Federation, 1997.

The Jurist 36/1–2 (1976). Entire issue on "The Church as Communion." Articles by J. H. Provost, M. A. Fahey, T. G. Bissonnette, and others.

Kaslyn, Robert J. *"Communion with the Church" and the Code of Canon Law*. Lewiston, N.Y.: Edwin Mellen, 1994.

Kasper, Walter. "The Church as Communion." In *Theology and Church*, 148–65. New York: Crossroad, 1989.

Klostermann, Ferdinand. *Gemeinde–Kirche der Zukunft: Thesen, Dienste, Modelle*. 2 vols. Freiburg: Herder, 1975.

Kress, Robert. *The Church: Communion, Sacrament, Communication*. New York: Paulist, 1985.

Lawler, Michael G., and Thomas J. Shanahan. *Church: A Spirited Communion*. Collegeville, Minn.: Liturgical Press, 1995.

Panikulam, George. *Koinonia in the New Testament: A Dynamic Expression of Christian Life*. Rome: Biblical Institute, 1979.

Ratzinger, Joseph. *Called to Communion: Understanding the Church Today*. San Francisco: Ignatius, 1996.

Reumann, John. "'Koinonia' in Scripture: Survey of Biblical Texts." In *On the Way to Fuller Koinonia*, edited by Thomas F. Best and Günther Gassmann, 37–69. Faith and Order Paper no. 166. Geneva: World Council of Churches, 1994. The article includes a lengthy bibliography.

Rigal, Jean. *L'ecclésiologie de communion: Son évolution historique et ses fondements*. Paris: Cerf, 1997.

Saier, Oskar. *"Communio" in der Lehre des zweiten Vatikanischen Konzils*. Munich: M. Hueber, 1973.

Schindler, David L. *Heart of the World, Center of the Church: Communio Ecclesiology, Liberalism, and Liberation*. Grand Rapids, Mich.: Wm. B. Eerdmans, 1996.

―――. *Chair de l'Eglise, chair du Christ: Aux sources de l'ecclésiologie de communion*. Paris: Cerf, 1992.

*Tillard, J.-M. R. *Church of Churches: The Ecclesiology of Communion*. Collegeville, Minn.: Liturgical Press, 1992. Preferably consult French original: *Église d'Églises*. Paris: Cerf, 1987.

Willebrands, Johannes. "Vatican II's Ecclesiology of Communion." *Origins* 17 (May 28, 1987): 27–33.

*Wood, Susan K. "Ecclesial Koinonia in Ecumenical Dialogues." *One in Christ* 30 (1994): 124–45.

30

BASIC ECCLESIAL COMMUNITIES

The authors in this section apply the idea of communion given above.

*Azevedo, Marcello deC. *Basic Ecclesial Communities in Brazil: The Challenge of a New Way of Being Church.* Washington, D.C.: Georgetown University, 1987.

Barbé, Dominique. *Demain, les communautés de base.* Paris: Cerf, 1970.

Barreiro, Alvaro. *Basic Ecclesial Communities: The Evangelization of the Poor.* Maryknoll, N.Y.: Orbis, 1982.

Bissonnette, Tomás G. "Comunidades Eclesiales de Base: Some Contemporary Attempts to Build Ecclesial Koinonia." *The Jurist* 36/1-2 (1976): 24–58.

Boff, Clodovis. "The Nature of Basic Christian Communities." In *Tensions between the Church of the First World and the Third World,* edited by Virgilio Elizondo and Norbert Greinacher, 53–58. Concilium, no. 144. New York: Seabury, 1981.

Boff, Leonardo. *Ecclesiogenesis: The Base Communities Reinvent the Church.* Maryknoll, N.Y.: Orbis, 1986.

Clark, Stephen B. *Building Christian Communities.* Notre Dame, Ind.: Ave Maria, 1972.

Cook, Guillermo. *The Expectation of the Poor: Latin American Basic Ecclesial Communities in Protestant Perspective.* Maryknoll, N.Y.: Orbis, 1985.

Costello, Gerald M. *Mission to Latin America.* Maryknoll, N.Y.: Orbis, 1979.

Cowan, Michael A., and Bernard J. Lee. *Conversation, Risk, and Conversion: The Inner and Public Life of Small Christian Communities.* Maryknoll, N.Y.: Orbis, 1997.

Delespesse, Max. *The Church Community: Leaven and Life Style.* Ottawa: Catholic Centre of St. Paul University, 1969.

Fraser, Ian, and Margaret Fraser. *Wind and Fire: The Spirit Reshapes the Church in Basic Christian Communities.* Dunblane, Scotland: Basic Communities Resource Center, 1986.

Latin American Documentation. *Basic Christian Communities.* Ladoc "Keyhole" Series. Washington, D.C.: USCC, 1976.

Lee, Bernard, and Michael A. Cowan. *Dangerous Memories: House Churches and Our American Story.* Kansas City, Mo.: Sheed & Ward, 1986.

Marins, José, and T. M. Trevisan. *Comunidades Eclesiales de Base.* Bogota: Paulinas, 1975.

National Federation of Priests' Councils. *Developing Basic Christian Communities: A Handbook.* Chicago: NFPC, 1979.

National Secretariat for Hispanic Affairs (USCC/NCCB). *Comunidades Eclesiales de Base en los Estados Unidos (Basic Ecclesial Communities: An Experience in the United States).* Liguori, Mo.: Liguori Publications, 1980.

O'Halloran, James. *Signs of Hope: Developing Small Christian Communities.* Maryknoll, N.Y.: Orbis, 1991.

*————. *Small Christian Communities: A Pastoral Companion.* Maryknoll, N.Y.: Orbis, 1996.

Perrin-Jassy, Marie France. *Basic Community in the African Churches.* Maryknoll, N.Y.: Orbis, 1973.

Pro Mundi Vita Bulletin, No. 81, 1980. This issue is devoted to basic Christian communities in the church.

Rausch, Thomas P. *Radical Christian Communities.* Collegeville, Minn.: Liturgical Press, 1990.

Torres, Sergio, and John Eagleson, eds. *The Challenge of Basic Christian Communities.* Maryknoll, N.Y.: Orbis, 1981.

Vandenakker, John Paul. *Small Christian Communities and the Parish.* Kansas City, Mo.: Sheed & Ward, 1994.

Vela, Jesús Andrés. *Comunidades de base, Conversión a qué?* 2nd ed. Bogota: Ediciones Paulinas, 1973.

THE CHURCH AS INSTITUTION AND STRUCTURE

References to a sociological analysis of the church are given below in section 33.

Baum, Gregory, and Andrew Greeley, eds. *The Church as Institution*. Concilium, no. 91. New York: Herder and Herder, 1974.

Congar, Yves M.-J. *Droit ancien et structures ecclésiales*. London: Variorum 1982. Contains several articles by Congar.

Defois, Gérard. *Le pouvoir dans l'Église: Analyse institutionnelle, historique et théologique*. Paris: Cerf, 1973.

Dombois, Hans. *Hierarchie: Grund und Grenze einer Umstrittenen Struktur*. Freiburg: Herder, 1971.

*Dulles, Avery. "Institution and Charism in the Church." In *A Church to Believe In*, chap. 2. New York: Crossroad, 1982.

L'Église: Institution et foi. Brussels: Publications des Facultés universitaires Saint-Louis, 1979.

*Granfield, Patrick. "The Church as Institution: A Reformulated Model." *Journal of Ecumenical Studies* 16 (1978): 425–47.

————. "The Church as *Societas Perfecta* in the Schemata of Vatican I." *Church History* 46 (1979): 431–46.

————. "The Rise and Fall of *Societas Perfecta*." In *May Church Ministers be Politicians?*, edited by Peter Huizing and Knut Walf, 3–8. Concilium, no. 157. New York: Seabury, 1982.

Jiménez-Urresti, Teodoro, ed. *Structures of the Church*. Concilium, no. 58. New York: Herder & Herder, 1970.

Kaufmann, Franz-Xaver. *Kirche Begreifen: Analysen und Thesen zur gesellschaftlichen Verfassung des Christentums*. Freiburg: Herder, 1979.

Kehl, Medard. *Kirche als Institution: Zur theologischen Begründung des institutionellen Charakters der Kirche in der neueren deutschsprachigen katholischen Ekklesiologie*. Frankfurt: J. Knecht, 1976.

*Küng, Hans. *Structures of the Church*. New York: T. Nelson, 1964. Paperback, Notre Dame, Ind.: University of Notre Dame, 1968.

Navarrette, Urban. "Potestas vicaria ecclesiae: Evolutio historica conceptus atque observationes attenta doctrina concilii Vaticani II." *Periodica de re morali, canonica, liturgica* 60 (1971): 415–86.

Pottmeyer, Hermann J., ed. *Kirche im Kontext der modernen Gesellschaft: Zur Strukturfrage der römisch-katholischen Kirche*. Freiburg: Katholische Akademie and Munich: Schnell & Steiner, 1989. Articles by H. J. Pottmeyer, F. X. Kaufmann, and others.

Pouvoirs: Revue française d'études constitutionnelles et politiques 17 (1981). Entire issue devoted to "Le pouvoir dans l'Église." Articles by G. Defois, E. Poulat, J. Gaudem, J.-L. Harouel, and others.

Reese, Thomas J. *Archbishop: Inside the Power Structure of the American Catholic Church*. San Francisco: Harper & Row, 1989.

————. *A Flock of Shepherds: The National Conference of Catholic Bishops*. Kansas City, Mo.: Sheed & Ward, 1992.

————. *Inside the Vatican: The Politics and Organization of the Catholic Church*. Cambridge, Mass. and London: Harvard University, 1996.

Schwartz, Reinhold. "De potestate propria ecclesiae." *Periodica de re morali, canonica, liturgica* 63 (1974): 429–55.

Walf, Knut. "Die katholische Kirche—eine 'societas perfecta.'" *Theologische Quartalschrift* 157 (1977): 107–18.

Zimmermann, Marie. "Stabilisation d'un modèle de société: La 'société parfaite.'" In *Structure sociale et Église*, 25–48. Strasbourg: CERDIC, 1981.

32

CONTINUITY, STRUCTURAL CHANGE, AND REFORM

Bernardin, Joseph, and Oscar H. Lipscomb. *Catholic Common Ground Initiative: Foundational Documents.* New York: Crossroad, 1997.

Bianchi, Eugene C., and Rosemary Radford Ruether, eds. *A Democratic Catholic Church: The Reconstruction of Roman Catholicism.* New York: Crossroad, 1992. Articles by J. Beal, H. Küng, J. P. Dolan, and others.

Chirico, Peter. "Priesthood, Eucharist, Hierarchy: Instantaneous or Emerging?" *Chicago Studies* 16 (1977): 265–77.

*Congar, Yves M.-J. *Vraie et fausse réforme dans l'Église.* Unam Sanctam, no. 20. Paris: Cerf, 1950. Rev. ed., 1968.

Dulles, Avery. "*Ius divinum* as an Ecumenical Problem." *Theological Studies* 38 (1977): 681–708. Reprinted in *A Church to Believe In*, chap. 6. New York: Crossroad, 1982.

―――. *The Resilient Church*, chap. 2, pp. 29–44. Garden City, N.Y.: Doubleday, 1977.

Fries, Heinrich. *Suffering from the Church: Renewal or Restoration?* Collegeville, Minn.: Liturgical Press, 1995.

Greinacher, Norbert, and Alois Müller, eds. *Ongoing Reform in the*

Church. Concilium, no. 73. New York: Herder and Herder, 1972.

Küng, Hans. *The Council, Reform, and Reunion*. New York: Sheed & Ward, 1962.

————. *Reforming the Church Today: Keeping Hope Alive*. New York: Crossroad, 1990.

Lafont, Ghislain. *Imaginer l'Église Catholique*. Paris: Cerf, 1995.

McBrien, Richard P. *The Remaking of the Church*. New York: Harper and Row, 1973.

O' Malley, John W. *Tradition and Transition: Historical Perspectives on Vatican II*. Wilmington, Del.: Michael Glazier, 1989.

Peter, Carl J. "Dimensions of *Jus Divinum* in Roman Catholic Theology." *Theological Studies* 34 (1973): 227–50.

*Rahner, Karl. "Basic Observations on the Subject of Changeable and Unchangeable Factors in the Church." In *Theological Investigations,* 14:3–23. New York: Crossroad, 1976.

————. "Reflections on the Concept of 'Jus Divinum' in Catholic Thought." In *Theological Investigations*, 5:219–43. New York: Crossroad, 1966.

Rigal, Jean. *L'Église: Obstacle et chemin vers Dieu*. 2nd ed. Paris: Cerf, 1984.

Tracy, David, Hans Küng, and Johann B. Metz, eds. *Toward Vatican II: The Work that Needs to Be Done*. New York: Seabury, 1978.

33

THE SOCIOLOGY OF THE CHURCH

The following titles are in addition to items listed under New Testament (section 8), Membership in the Church (section 25), and The Church as Institution and Structure (section 31).

Afonso, Meneo A. *What is the Nature of Authority in the Church?* Lanham, Md.: University Press of America, 1996.

Baum, Gregory. "The Impact of Sociology on Catholic Theology." *Proceedings of the Catholic Theological Society of America* 30 (1975): 1–29. Responses by Patrick J. Burns and Mary I. Buckley (pp. 31–47).

Berger, Peter L. *The Noise of Solemn Assemblies.* Garden City, N.Y.: Doubleday, 1961.

———. *A Rumor of Angels.* Garden City, N.Y.: Doubleday, 1970.

———. *The Sacred Canopy*: *Elements of a Sociological Theory of Religion.* Garden City, N.Y.: Doubleday, 1967.

Burns, Patrick J. "Precarious Reality: Ecclesiological Reflections on Peter Berger." *Theology Digest* 21 (1973): 322–33.

Coleman, John A. *An American Strategic Theology.* New York: Paulist, 1982.

Fichter, Joseph. *Organization Man in the Church.* Cambridge: Schenkman, 1974.

———. *Southern Parish.* Chicago: University of Chicago, 1951.

Gill, Robin, ed. *Theology and Sociology: A Reader.* London: Geoffrey Chapman; New York and Mahwah, N.J.: Paulist, 1987.

Greeley, Andrew M. *The American Catholic: A Social Portrait.* New York: Basic Books, 1977.

———. *The Communal Catholic: A Personal Manifesto.* New York: Seabury, 1976.

———. *The Denominational Society: A Sociological Approach to Religion in America.* Glenview, Ill.: Scott, Foresman, 1972.

*Gustafson, James M. *Treasure in Earthen Vessels: The Church as a Human Community.* New York: Harper & Row, 1961.

Houtart, François, and Rémy, Jean. *Église et société en mutation.* Paris: Mame, 1969.

Kee, Howard Clark. *Christian Origins in Sociological Perspective.* Philadelphia: Westminster, 1980.

*Komonchak, Joseph A. "Ecclesiology and Social Theory: A Methodological Essay." *Thomist* 45 (1981): 262–83.

Martin, David A. *The Breaking of the Image: A Sociology of Christian Theory and Practice.* New York: St. Martin, 1980.

Moberg, David O. *The Church as Social Institution: The Sociology of American Religion.* Englewood Cliffs, N.J.: Prentice-Hall, 1962.

Niebuhr, H. Richard. *The Social Sources of Denominationalism.* New York: H. Holt, 1927. Reprint, New York: Meridian Books, 1957; New American Library, 1980.

O'Dea, Thomas F. *Sociology and the Study of Religion.* New York: Basic Books, 1970.

Richey, Russell E., ed. *Denominationalism*. Nashville, Tenn.: Abingdon, 1977.

Troeltsch, Ernst. *The Social Teaching of the Christian Churches*. 2 vols. New York: Macmillan, 1930. Reprint, Chicago: University of Chicago, 1981.

Varacalli, Joseph A. *Toward the Establishment of Liberal Catholicism in America*. Washington, D.C.: University Press of America, 1983.

Ven, Johannes A. van der. *Ecclesiology in Context*. Grand Rapids, Mich.: Wm. B. Eerdmans, 1996.

Weber, Max. *From Max Weber*. Edited by H. H. Gerth and C. W. Mills. New York: Oxford University, 1946.

Wilson, Bryan R. *Religion in Sociological Perspective*. New York and Oxford: Oxford University, 1982.

Winter, Gibson. *The Suburban Captivity of the Churches*. New York: Doubleday, 1961.

Zimmermann, Marie. *Structure sociale et Église*. Strasbourg: CERDIC, 1981.

34

FREEDOM AND PARTICIPATION IN THE CHURCH

Bassett, William, and Peter Huizing, eds. *Judgment in the Church.* Concilium, no. 107. New York: Herder and Herder, 1977.

Corecco, Eugenio, et al. *Les droits fondamentaux du chrétien dans l'Église et dans la société.* Fribourg: Éditions universitaires, 1982.

Coriden, James A., ed. *We the People of God: A Study of Constitutional Government in the Church.* Huntington, Ind.: Canon Law Society of America, 1968.

Curran, Charles E., and Robert E. Hunt. *Dissent in and for the Church.* New York: Sheed & Ward, 1970.

Drane, James F. *Authority and Institution: A Study in Church Crisis.* Milwaukee, Wis.: Bruce, 1969.

González Faus, José I. *Where the Spirit Breathes: Prophetic Dissent in the Church.* Maryknoll, N.Y.: Orbis, 1989.

*Granfield, Patrick. *Ecclesial Cybernetics: A Study of Democracy in the Church.* New York: Macmillan, 1973.

Küng, Hans. *Freedom Today.* New York: Sheed & Ward, 1966.

Leys, Ad. *Ecclesiological Impacts on the Principle of Subsidiarity*. Kampen: Kok, 1995.

Moltmann, Jürgen, and Hans Küng, eds. *Who Has the Say in the Church?* Concilium, no. 148. New York: Seabury, 1981.

Müller, Alois, ed. *Democratization of the Church*. Concilium, no. 63. New York: Herder and Herder, 1971.

*Nichols, Terence L. *That All May Be One: Hierarchy and Participation in the Church*. Collegeville, Minn.: Liturgical Press, 1997.

Orna, Mary Virginia. *Cybernetics, Society, and the Church*. Dayton, Ohio: Pflaum, 1969.

Rahner, Karl. "Freedom in the Church." In *Theological Investigations*, 2:89–107. Baltimore: Helicon, 1963.

———. *Free Speech in the Church*. New York: Sheed & Ward, 1960.

Swidler, Leonard. *Freedom in the Church*. Dayton, Ohio: Pflaum, 1969.

35

THE PAPACY

On this topic also see section 15 (Vatican Council I) and section 38 (Infallibility).

Alberigo, Giuseppe, ed. *Renouveau ecclésial et service papal à la fin du XXe siècle*. Concilium, no. 108 (French edition). Paris: Beauchesne, 1975.

Allmen, Jean Jacques von. *La primauté de Pierre et Paul: Remarques d'un Protestant*. Fribourg: Éditions universitaires, 1977.

Anglican-Roman Catholic International Commission. *The Final Report*. Washington, D.C.: USCC, 1982.

Arbeitsgemeinschaft ökumenischer Universitätsinstitut. *Papsttum als ökumenische Frage*. Munich: Kaiser; Mainz: Matthias-Grünewald, 1979.

*Balthasar, Hans Urs von. *The Office of Peter and the Structure of the Church*. San Francisco: Ignatius, 1986.

Batiffol, Pierre. *Cathedra Petri: Études d'histoire ancienne de l'Église*. Unam Sanctam, no. 4. Paris: Cerf, 1938.

Brandenburg, Albert, and Hans Jörg Urban, eds. *Petrus und Papst*. Münster: Aschendorff, 1977.

Brown, Raymond E., Karl P. Donfried, and John Reumann, eds.

Peter in the New Testament. Minneapolis: Augsburg; New York: Paulist, 1973.

Buckley, Michael J. *Papal Primacy and the Episcopate: Towards a Relational Understanding.* New York: Crossroad, 1998.

Burn-Murdoch, Hector. *The Development of the Papacy.* New York: Praeger, 1954.

Congar, Yves. *Église et papauté: Regards historiques.* Paris, Cerf, 1994.

Cooke, Bernard, ed. *The Papacy and the Church in the United States.* New York and Mahwah, N.J.: Paulist, 1989. Articles by B. Tierney, G. Fogarty, F. McManus, and others.

Cullmann, Oscar. *Peter: Disciple, Apostle, Martyr.* London: SCM, 1961.

Denzler, Georg, ed. *Das Papsttum in der Diskussion.* Regensburg: Pustet, 1974.

Dionne, J. Robert. *The Papacy and the Church: A Study of Praxis and Reception in Ecumenical Perspective.* New York: Philosophical Library, 1987.

Dix, Gregory. *Jurisdiction in the Early Church: Episcopal and Papal.* London: Church and Literature Association, 1975.

Empie, Paul C., and T. Austin Murphy, eds. *Papal Primacy and the Universal Church.* Lutherans and Catholics in Dialogue, vol. 5. Minneapolis: Augsburg, 1974.

Eno, Robert B. *The Rise of the Papacy.* Wilmington, Del.: Michael Glazier, 1990.

Ernst, Cornelius. "The Primacy of Peter: Theology and Ideology." *New Blackfriars* 50 (1969): 347–55, 399–404.

Farmer, William R., and Roch Kereszty. *Peter and Paul in the Church of Rome: The Ecumenical Potential of a Forgotten Perspective.* New York and Mahwah, N.J.: Paulist, 1990.

Franzen, August, and Remigius Bäumer. *Papstgeschichte: Das Petrusamt in seiner Idee und seiner geschichtlichen Verwirklichung in der Kirche.* Freiburg: Herder, 1974.

Fuellenbach, John. *Ecclesiastical Office and the Primacy of Rome: An Evaluation of Recent Theological Discussion of First Clement.* Washington, D.C.: Catholic University of America, 1980.

Galvin, John P. "Papal Primacy in Contemporary Roman Catholic Theology." *Theological Studies* 47 (1986): 653–67.

Garuti, Adriano. *S. Pietro unico titolare del primato: A proposito del decreto del S. Uffizio del 24 gennaio 1647.* Bologna: Edizioni Francescane, 1993.

*Granfield, Patrick. "Cum Petro et Sub Petro: Episcopacy and Primacy." *The Jurist* 54 (1994): 591–604.

———. *The Limits of the Papacy: Authority and Autonomy in the Church.* New York: Crossroad, 1987.

———. "Papacy." In *The Encyclopedia of Religion*, 11:171–83. New York: Macmillan, 1987.

*———. *The Papacy in Transition.* Garden City, N.Y.: Doubleday, 1980. Extensive bibliography.

Hardt, Michael. *Papsttum und Ökumene: Ansätze eines Neuverständnisses für einen Papstprimat in der protestantischen Theologie des 20. Jahrhunderts.* Paderborn: F. Schöningh, 1981.

Holmes, J. Derek. *The Papacy in the Modern World: 1914–1978.* New York: Crossroad, 1981.

———. *The Triumph of the Holy See: A Short History of the Papacy in the Nineteenth Century.* London: Burns & Oates; Shepherdstown, W. Va.: Patmos, 1978.

Jalland, Trevor Gervase. *The Church and the Papacy.* London: SPCK, 1944.

Kelly, J. N. D. *The Oxford Dictionary of the Popes.* Oxford and New York: Oxford University, 1986.

Klausnitzer, Wolfgang. *Das Paptsamt im Disput zwischen Lutheranen und Katholiken.* Innsbruck: Tyrolia, 1987.

Küng, Hans, ed. *Papal Ministry in the Church.* Concilium, no 64. New York: Herder and Herder, 1971.

Lehmann, Karl, ed. *Das Petrusamt: Geschichtliche Stationen seines Verständnisses und gegenwärtige Positionen.* Munich: Schnell & Steiner, 1982. Articles by R. Pesch, H. J. Pottmeyer, and others.

Liber Pontificalis. The Book of Pontiffs. Translated by R. Davis. Liverpool: Liverpool University, 1989.

Maccarrone, Michele. *Il primato del vescovo di Roma nel primo millennio: Ricerche e testimonianze.* Vatican City: Libreria Editrice Vaticana, 1991.

———. *Vicarius Christi: Storia del titolo papale.* Rome: Facultas theologica pontificii athenaei lateranensis, 1952.

MacEoin, Gary, ed. *The Papacy and the People of God.* Maryknoll, N.Y.: Orbis, 1998. (Articles by H. Cox, F. X. Murphy, G. Zizola, and others.)

Markus, Robert, and Eric John. *Pastors or Princes: A New Look at the Papacy and Hierarchy.* Washington, D.C.: Corpus, 1968.

May, Georg. *Ego N. N. Catholicae Ecclesiae Episcopus: Entstehung, Entwicklung und Bedeutung einer Unterschriftsformel im Hinblick auf den Universalepiskopat des Päpstes.* Berlin: Duncker & Humbolt, 1995.

McBrien, Richard P. *Lives of the Popes: The Pontiffs from St. Peter to John Paul II.* San Francisco: Harper, 1997.

*McCord, Peter J., ed. *A Pope for All Christians?* New York: Paulist, 1976. Articles by A. Dulles, J. Burgess, J. Meyendorff, J. R. Nelson, and others.

Meyendorff, John, et al. *The Primacy of Peter in the Orthodox Church*. Leighton Buzzard, U.K.: Faith, 1963. Reprint, 1973.

Miller, J. Michael. *The Divine Right of the Papacy in Recent Ecumenical Theology*. Rome: Gregoriana, 1980.

———. *The Shepherd and the Rock: Origins, Development, and Mission of the Papacy*. Huntington, Ind.: Our Sunday Visitor, 1995.

———. *What Are They Saying about Papal Primacy?* New York: Paulist, 1983.

Mund, Hans-Joachim, ed. *Das Petrusamt in der gegenwärtigen Diskussion*. Paderborn: F. Schöningh, 1976.

Mussner, Franz. *Petrus und Paulus–Pole der Einheit*. Freiburg: Herder, 1976.

Noble, Thomas F. X. *The Republic of St. Peter: The Birth of the Papal State, 680–825*. Philadelphia: University of Pennsylvania, 1984.

Ohlig, Karl-Heinz. *Why We Need the Pope*. St. Meinrad, Ind.: Abbey, 1975.

Pennington, Kenneth. *Pope and Bishops: The Papal Monarchy in the Twelfth and Thirteenth Centuries*. Philadelphia: University of Pennsylvania, 1984.

Pottmeyer, Hermann Josef. *Towards a Papacy in Communion: Perspectives from Vatican Councils I and II*. New York: Crossroad, 1998.

Quinn, John R. "Considering the Papacy." Oxford Lecture. *Origins* 26 (July 18, 1996): 119–28.

Satgé, John de. *Peter and the Single Church*. London: SPCK, 1981.

*Schatz, Klaus. *Papal Primacy: From its Origins to the Present*. Collegeville, Minn.: Liturgical Press, 1996.

Schimmelpfennig, Bernhard. *The Papacy*. New York: Columbia University, 1992. A history of the papacy from the beginning to 1534.

Sherrard, Philip. *Church, Papacy, and Schism: A Theological Inquiry*. London: SPCK, 1978.

Thils, Gustave. *Primauté et infaillibilité du pontife Romain à Vatican I et autres études d'ecclésiologie*. Leuven: Leuven University and Uitgeverij Peeters, 1989.

————. *La primauté pontificale: Le doctrine de Vatican I*. Gembloux: J. Duculot, 1972.

*Tillard, Jean M. R. *The Bishop of Rome*. Wilmington, Del.: Michael Glazier, 1983.

Ullmann, Walter. *The Growth of Papal Government in the Middle Ages*. 3rd ed. London: Methuen, 1970.

————. *A Short History of the Papacy in the Middle Ages*. London: Methuen, 1972.

Zagano, Phyllis, and Terrence W. Tilley. *The Exercise of the Primacy: Continuing the Dialogue*. New York: Crossroad, 1998. Responses to Archbishop Quinn's Oxford lecture (see above) by R. Scott Appleby, E. A. Johnson, T. P. Rausch and others.

36

EPISCOPACY AND COLLEGIALITY

Anciaux, Paul. *The Episcopate in the Church.* Dublin: Gill & Sons, 1965.

Bertrams, Wilhelm. *The Papacy, the Episcopacy, and Collegiality.* Westminster, Md.: Newman, 1964.

Betti, Umberto. *La dottrina sull'episcopato del capitolo III della costitutione dommatica Lumen Gentium.* Rome: Città nuova, 1968.

Bouëssé, Humbert, and André Mandouze, eds. *L'évêque dans l'Égise du Christ.* Bruges: Desclée De Brouwer, 1963.

Colson, Jean. *L'épiscopat catholique: Collégialité et primauté dans les trois premiers siècles.* Unam Sanctam, no. 43. Paris: Cerf, 1963.

―――. *L'évêque dans les communautés primitives.* Unam Sanctam, no. 21. Paris: Cerf, 1951.

Congar, Yves M.-J. *Ministères et communion ecclésiale.* Paris: Cerf, 1971.

*Congar, Yves M.-J., et al. *La collégialité épiscopale.* Unam Sanctam, no. 52. Paris: Cerf, 1965.

Congar, Yves M.-J., and Bernard-Dominique Dupuy, eds. *L'épisco-pat et l'Église universelle*. Unam Sanctam, no. 39. Paris: Cerf, 1962.

Cunningham, Agnes. *The Bishop in the Church: Patristic Texts on the Role of Episkopos*. Wilmington, Del.: Michael Glazier, 1985.

Dóriga, Enrique L. *Jerarquía, infalibilidad, y comunión intereclesial*. Barcelona: Herder, 1973.

Fagiolo, Vincenzo, and Gino Concetti. *La collegialità episcopale per il futuro della chiesa*. Florence: Vallecchi, 1969.

Fogarty, Gerald P., ed. *Patterns of Episcopal Leadership*. New York: Macmillan, 1989.

Gagnebet, Rosarius. "De duplici subiecto unicae potestatis supremae." In *Acta congressus internationalis de theologia Concilii Vaticani Secundi*, edited by A. Schönmetzer, 118–28. Vatican City: Typis Polyglottis Vaticanis, 1968.

Gaudemet, J., et al., eds. *Les élections dans l'Église latine des origines au XVIe siècle*. Paris: F. Lenore, 1979.

Ghirlanda, Gianfranco. *"Hierarchica communio": Significato della formula nella Lumen Gentium*. Rome: Gregoriana, 1980.

Grootaers, Jan, ed. *Primauté et collégialité: Le dossier de Gérard Philips sur la Nota Explicativa Praevia*. Leuven: Leuven University and Uitgeverij Peeters, 1986.

Groupe des Dombes. "The Episcopal Ministry." *One in Christ* 14 (1978): 267–88.

Hastings, Adrian, ed. *Bishops and Writers: Aspects of the Evolution of Modern English Catholicism*. Wheathampstead, Hertfordshire: Anthony Clarke, 1977.

Howell, Patrick J., and Gary Chamberlain, eds. *Empowering Authority: The Charisms of Episcopacy and Primacy in the Church Today*. Kansas City, Mo.: Sheed & Ward, 1990.

Huizing, Peter, and Knut Walf, eds. *Electing Our Own Bishops*. Concilium, no. 137. Edinburgh: T & T Clark; New York: Seabury, 1980.

Istituto Paolo VI. *Paolo VI e la collegialità episcopale*. Brescia: Istituto Paolo VI, 1995.

Lécuyer, Joseph. *Études sur la collégialité épiscopale*. Lyon: Mappus, 1964.

Mazzoni, Giampietro. *La collegialità episcopale: Tra teologia e diritto canonico*. Bologna: Dehoniane, 1986.

McBrien, Richard. "Collegiality: The State of the Question." In *The Once and Future Church*, edited by James A. Coriden, 1–24. Staten Island, N.Y.: Alba House, 1971.

Minnerath, Roland. *Le pape: Évêque universel ou premier des évêques?* Paris: Beauchesne, 1978.

Moore, Peter, ed. *Bishops but What Kind? Reflections on Episcopacy*. London: SPCK, 1982.

Mörsdorf, Klaus. "Decree on the Bishops' Pastoral Office in the Church." In *Commentary on the Documents of Vatican II*, edited by Herbert Vorgrimler, 2:165–300. New York: Herder and Herder, 1968.

*Murphy, Charles M. "Collegiality: An Essay Toward Better Understanding." *Theological Studies* 46 (1985): 38–49.

National Conference of Catholic Bishops. *A Manual for Bishops: Rights and Responsibilities of Diocesan Bishops in the Revised Code of Canon Law*. Rev. ed. Washington, D.C.: USCC, 1992.

———. *The Ministry of Bishops: Papers from the Collegeville Assembly*. Washington, D.C.: USCC, 1982. Articles by J. Dearden, J. A. Hickey, R. F. Sanchez, T. J. Gumbleton, W. D. Borders, R. G. Weakland, and G. B. Hume.

Provost, James, and Knut Walf, eds. *Collegiality Put to the Test*. Concilium 1990/4. London: SCM; Philadelphia: Trinity

Press International, 1990. Articles by H. Rikhof, J. Grootaers, D. Valentini, and others.

Rahner, Karl. *Bishops: Their Status and Function*. London: Burns & Oates, 1964.

————. "The Episcopal Office." In *Theological Investigations*, 6:313–60. New York: Crossroad, 1969. See also similar articles in vols. 10 and 14.

*Rahner, Karl, and Joseph Ratzinger. *Episcopate and Primacy*. New York: Herder and Herder, 1962.

Ratzinger, Joseph. "The Pastoral Implications of Episcopal Collegiality." In *The Church and Mankind*, edited by Edward Schillebeeckx, 39–67. Concilium, no. 1. Glen Rock, N.J.: Paulist, 1965.

Sacred Congregation for Bishops. *Directory on the Pastoral Ministry of Bishops*. Ottawa: Canadian Catholic Conference, 1974.

Schauf, Heribert. *Das Leitungsamt der Bischöfe: Zur Textgeschichte der Konstitution "Lumen Gentium" des II. Vatikanischen Konzils*. Munich: F. Schöningh, 1975.

Stanley, David M. "The New Testament Basis for the Concept of Collegiality." *Theological Studies* 25 (1964): 197–216.

*Suenens, Léon Joseph. *Coresponsibility in the Church*. New York: Herder and Herder, 1968.

Swidler, Arlene, and Leonard Swidler, eds. *Bishops and People*. Philadelphia: Westminster, 1970.

Thils, Gustave. *Primauté pontificale et prérogatives épiscopales: "Potestas ordinaria" au Concile du Vatican*. Louvain: E. Warny, 1961.

Torrell, Jean-Pierre. *La théologie de l'épiscopat au premier Concile du Vatican*. Unam Sanctam, no. 37. Paris: Cerf, 1961.

Tuell, Jack M., and Roger W. Fjeld, eds. *Episcopacy: Lutheran–United Methodist Dialogue II*. Minneapolis: Augsburg, 1991.

Veuillot, P., and Yves M.-J. Congar. *La charge pastorale des évêques: Décret "Christus Dominus."* Unam Sanctam, no. 71. Paris: Cerf, 1969. Articles by W. Onclin, H. Legrand, F. Boulard, and others.

37

THE TEACHING OFFICE

Alfaro, Juan. "Theology's Role Regarding the Magisterium." *Theology Digest* 25 (1977): 212–16. Abstracted from *Gregorianum* 57 (1976): 39–79.

*Boyle, John P. *Church Teaching Authority: Historical and Theological Studies*. Notre Dame, Ind.: University of Notre Dame, 1995.

Chicago Studies 17 (1978). Entire issue devoted to the Magisterium. Articles by E. LaVerdiere, J. E. Lynch, Y. M.-J. Congar, A. Dulles, R. E. Brown, and others.

Congar, Yves M.-J. "Bref historique des formes du 'magistère' et de ses relations avec les docteurs." *Revue des sciences philosophiques et théologiques* 60 (1976): 99–112. English version in C. E. Curran and R. A. McCormick, *The Magisterium and Morality*, 314–31. New York: Paulist, 1982.

Congar, Yves M.-J., et al. *Les théologiens et l'Église*. Paris: Beauchesne, 1980.

Congregation for the Doctrine of the Faith. *Instruction on the Ecclesial Vocation of the Theologian (Donum Veritatis)*. Vatican City: Libreria Editrice Vaticana, 1990. Also found in *Origins* 20 (July 5, 1990): 117–26.

*Curran, Charles E., and R. A. McCormick, eds. *Dissent in the

Church. Readings in Moral Theology, no. 6. New York and Mahwah, N.J.: Paulist, 1988.

————, eds. *The Magisterium and Morality*. Readings in Moral Theology, no. 3. New York: Paulist, 1982.

Descamps, A. L. "Théologie et magistère." *Ephemerides theologicae lovanienses* 52 (1976): 82–133.

Dulles, Avery. "The Magisterium in History: Theological Considerations." In *A Church to Believe In*, chap. 7. New York: Crossroad, 1982.

————. *The Survival of Dogma*. Garden City, N.Y.: Doubleday, 1971.

————. "The Two Magisteria: An Interim Reflection." In *A Church to Believe In*, chap. 8. New York: Crossroad, 1982.

Empie, Paul C., T. Austin Murphy, and Joseph A. Burgess, eds. *Teaching Authority and Infallibility in the Church*. Lutherans and Catholics in Dialogue, vol. 6. Minneapolis: Augsburg, 1978.

Eno, Robert B. *Teaching Authority in the Early Church*. Wilmington, Del.: Michael Glazier; Collegeville, Minn.: Liturgical Press, 1984. A selection of patristic texts.

Ford, John C., and Germain Grisez. "Contraception and the Infallibility of the Ordinary Magisterium." *Theological Studies* 39 (1978): 258–312.

*Gaillardetz, Richard R. *Teaching With Authority: A Theology of the Magisterium in the Church*. Collegeville, Minn.: Liturgical Press, 1997.

International Theological Commission. *Theses on the Relationship between the Ecclesiastical Magisterium and Theology*. Washington, D.C.: USCC, 1977.

Irish Theological Quarterly 43 (1976): 225–92. Issue on Magisterium with articles by C. B. Daly, R. B. Coffy, K. Wojtyla, and A. Poma.

John Paul II. *Ad Tuendam Fidem*. Apostolic Letter, *Origins* 28 (July 16, 1998): 113, 115–16.

Kern, Walter, ed. *Die Theologie und das Lehramt*. Freiburg: Herder, 1982. Articles by M. Seckler, W. Kasper, P. Eicher, and others.

Komonchak, Joseph A. "*Humanae vitae* and its Reception: Ecclesiological Reflections." *Theological Studies* 39 (1978): 221–57.

———. "Ordinary Papal Magisterium and Religious Assent." In *Contraception: Authority and Dissent,* edited by C. E. Curran, 101–26. New York: Herder and Herder, 1969.

May, William W., ed. *Vatican Authority and American Catholic Dissent: The Curran Case and Its Consequences*. New York: Crossroad, 1987. Articles by C. E. Curran, R. A. McCormick, W. E. May, and others.

McCormick, Richard A. "The Magisterium and Theologians." *Proceedings of the Catholic Theological Society of America* 24 (1969): 239–54.

McKenzie, John L. *Authority in the Church*. New York: Sheed & Ward, 1966.

Morrisey, Francis G. *The Canonical Significance of Papal and Curial Pronouncements*. Washington, D.C.: Canon Law Society of America, 1981.

National Conference of Catholic Bishops. "The Teaching Ministry of the Diocesan Bishop: A Pastoral Reflection." *Origins* 21 (Jan. 2, 1992): 473, 475–92.

Naud, André. *Le magistère incertain*. Montreal: Fides, 1987.

O'Donovan, Leo J., ed. *Cooperation between Theologians and the Ecclesiastical Magisterium*. A Report of the Joint Committee of CLSA and CTSA. Washington, D.C.: CLSA, 1982. Articles by J. A. Alesandro, J. P. Boyle, R. J. Carlson, P. Granfield, J. Nilson, and J. H. Provost. This same committee also published "Doctrinal Responsibilities: Procedures for Promoting Cooperation and Resolving Disputes between Bishops and Theologians." For text, see Canon Law Society of America, *Proceedings of the Forty-Fifth Annual Convention* (1983), 261–84 (Washington, D.C.: CLSA, 1984) and *Proceedings of the Catholic Theological Society of America* 39 (1984): 209–34. A revised edition was adopted by the National Conference of Catholic Bishops: "Doctrinal Responsibilities: Approaches to Promoting Cooperation and Resolving Misunderstandings between Bishops and Theologians." *Origins* 19 (June 29, 1989): 97, 99–110.

Orsy, Ladislas. *The Church: Learning and Teaching. Magisterium, Assent, Dissent, Academic Freedom.* Wilmington, Del.: Michael Glazier, 1987.

Rahner, Karl. "Magisterium." In *Sacramentum Mundi,* 3:351–58. New York: Herder and Herder, 1968. Reprinted in *Encyclopedia of Theology: The Concise Sacramentum Mundi,* 871–80. New York: Seabury, 1975.

Recherches de science religieuse 71 (1983): 1–308. Two issues devoted to the Magisterium: "Le magistère: institution et fonctionnements." Articles by J. Moingt, J. Doré, C. Pairault, J. Hoffmann, and others.

Riedl, Alfons. *Die kirchliche Lehrautorität in Fragen der Moral nach den Aussagen des Ersten Vatikanischen Konzils.* Freiburg: Herder, 1979.

Sanks, T. Howland. *Authority in the Church: A Study in Changing Paradigms.* Missoula, Mont.: Scholars Press, 1974.

Seckler, Max, ed. *Lehramt und Theologie.* Düsseldorf: Patmos, 1981.

*Sullivan, Francis A. *Creative Fidelity: Weighing and Interpreting Documents of the Magisterium.* New York and Mahwah, N.J.: Paulist, 1996.

————. *Magisterium: Teaching Office in the Catholic Church*. New York: Paulist, 1983.

————. "On the Infallibility of the Episcopal College in the Ordinary Exercise of its Teaching Office." In *Acta congressus internationalis de theologia Concilii Vaticani Secundi*, edited by A. Schönmetzer, 189–95. Vatican City: Typis Polyglottis Vaticanis, 1968.

Le Supplément, no. 133 (Mai 1980). Entire issue devoted to the Magisterium: "La régulation de la foi." Articles by J. Guillet, A. Dumas, Y. M.-J. Congar, C. Duquoc, and others.

Swidler, Leonard, and Piet Fransen, eds. *Authority in the Church and the Schillebeeckx Case*. New York: Crossroad, 1982. Articles by E. Schillebeeckx, P. Schoonenberg, T. I. Jiménez-Urresti, and others. Also published in *Journal of Ecumenical Studies* 19/2 (1982).

Todd, John M., ed. *Problems of Authority*. Baltimore: Helicon, 1962.

38

INFALLIBILITY

This section lists works specifically concerned with infallibility. It is in addition to the materials found in the preceding section. Some further titles are listed under section 15 (Vatican Council I) and section 35 (The Papacy).

Bantle, Franz Xaver. *Unfehlbarkeit der Kirche in Aufklärung und Romantik: Eine dogmengeschichtliche Untersuchung für die Zeit der Wende vom 18. zum 19. Jahrhundert.* Freiburg: Herder, 1976.

Bermejo, Luis M. *Infaillibility on Trial: Church, Conciliarity, and Communion.* Westminster, Md.: Christian Classics, 1992.

Butler, Basil Christopher. *The Church and Infallibility.* London: Sheed & Ward, 1954. Rev. ed., 1969.

Castelli, Enrico, ed. *L'infaillibilité: Son aspect philosophique et théologique.* Paris: Aubier, 1970.

Chirico, Peter. *Infallibility: Crossroads of Doctrine.* Kansas City, Mo.: Sheed, Andrews, & McMeel, 1977. Reprinted with a foreword by B. C. Butler and a new introduction by the author, Wilmington, Del.: Michael Glazier, 1983.

Costigan, Richard F. "The Consensus of the Church." *Theological Studies* 51 (1990): 25–48.

De doctrina Concilii Vaticani Primi: Studia selecta annis 1948–1964 scripta denuo edita cum centesimus annus compleretur ab eodem inchoata Concilio, 285–575. Vatican City: Libreria Editrice Vaticana, 1969. Compiled by Roger Piubert and others. Contains reprints of previously published articles by J.-P. Torrell, G. Dejaifve, G. Thils, and A. Chavasse.

Ford, John T. "Infallibility: A Review of Recent Studies." *Theological Studies* 40 (1979): 273–305.

*Gaillardetz, Richard R. *Witness to the Faith: Community, Infallibility, and the Ordinary Magisterium*. New York and Mahwah, N.J.: Paulist, 1992.

Gasser, Vinzenz. *The Gift of Infallibility: The Official Relatio on Infallibility of Bishop Gasser at Vatican Council I*. Translation and commentary by James T. O'Connor. Boston: St. Paul Editions, 1986.

Goulder, M. D. *Infallibility in the Church: An Anglican–Catholic Dialogue*. London: Darton, Longman & Todd, 1968.

Horst, Ulrich. *Papst-Konzil-Unfehlbarkeit*. Mainz: Matthias-Grünewald, 1978.

———. *Unfehlbarkeit und Geschichte: Studien zur Urlfehlbarkeitsdiskussion von Melchior Cano bis zum I. Vatikanischen Konzil*. Mainz: Matthias-Grünewald, 1982.

Journal of Ecumenical Studies 8 (1971): 751–871. Devoted to infallibility. Articles by L. Swidler, J. T. Ford, B. Tierney, and others.

Kirvan, John J., ed. *The Infallibility Debate*. New York: Paulist, 1971.

Klausnitzer, Wolfgang. *Päpstliche Unfehlbarkeit bei Newman und Döllinger: Ein historisch-systematischer Vergleich*. Innsbruck: Tyrolia, 1980.

Küng, Hans. *Fehlbar? Eine Bilanz*. Zurich: Benziger, 1973. Extensive bibliography on the "infallibility debate."

———. *Infallible? An Unresolved Inquiry.* Rev. ed. New York: Continuum, 1994.

———. *Structures of the Church.* New York: T. Nelson, 1964. Paperback, Notre Dame, Ind.: University of Notre Dame, 1968.

Lindbeck, George A. *Infallibility.* Milwaukee, Wis.: Marquette University Theology Department, 1972.

O'Gara, Margaret. *Triumph in Defeat: Infallibility, Vatican I, and the French Minority Bishops.* Washington, D.C.: Catholic University of America, 1988.

Page, John R. *What Will Dr. Newman Do? John Henry Newman and Papal Infallibility, 1865–1875.* Collegeville, Minn.: Liturgical Press, 1994.

Pottmeyer, Hermann Josef. *Unfehlbarkeit und Souveränität: Die päpstliche Unfehlbarkeit im System der ultramontanen Ekklesiologie des 19. Jahrhunderts.* Mainz: Matthias-Grünewald, 1975.

Rahner, Karl, ed. *Zum Problem Unfehlbarkeit: Antworten auf die Anfrage von Hans Küng.* Freiburg: Herder, 1971.

Rousseau, Olivier, et al. *L'infaillibilité de l'Église.* Gembloux: Chevetogne, 1963.

Schatz, Klaus. *Kirchenbild und päpstliche Unfehlbarkeit bei den deutschsprachigen Minoritätsbischöfen auf dem 1. Vatikanum.* Rome: Gregoriana, 1975.

Tekippe, Terry J., ed. *Papal Infallibility: An Application of Lonergan's Theological Method.* Washington, D.C.: University Press of America, 1983.

*Thils, Gustave. *L'infaillibilité pontificale: Sources, conditions, limites.* Gembloux: J. Duculot, 1969.

Tierney, Brian. *Origins of Papal Infallibility 1150–1350.* Leiden: Brill, 1972.

39

COUNCILS: ECUMENICAL, NATIONAL, AND DIOCESAN

Botte, Bernard, et al. *Le Concile et les conciles*. Chevetogne: Chevetogne, 1960. See especially articles by P.-T. Camelot and Y. M.-J. Congar.

Burke, Mary, and Eugene F. Hemrick. *Building the Local Church: Shared Responsibility in Diocesan Pastoral Councils*. Washington, D.C.: USCC, 1984.

Burns, Patrick J. "Communion, Councils, and Collegiality: Some Catholic Reflections." In *Papal Primacy and the Universal Church*, edited by P. C. Empie and T. A. Murphy, 151–72. Minneapolis: Augsburg, 1974.

Congar, Yves M.-J. "The Church as an Assembly and the Church as Essentially Conciliar." In *One, Holy, Catholic, and Apostolic*, edited by Herbert Vorgrimler, 44–48. London: Sheed & Ward, 1968.

———. "Concile." *Catholicisme*, 2:1439–43. Paris: Letouzey, 1950.

*———. "La réception comme réalité ecclésiologique." *Revue des sciences philosophiques et théologiques* 56 (1972): 364–403. See also abridged version in *Election and Consensus in the Church*, edited by Giuseppe Alberigo and Anton Weiler,

43–68. Concilium, no. 77. New York: Herder and Herder, 1972.

Dvornik, Francis. *The Ecumenical Councils*. 20th Century Encyclopedia of Catholicism, vol. 82. New York: Hawthorn Books, 1961.

Eno, Robert B. "Pope and Council: The Patristic Origins." *Science et esprit* 28 (1976): 183–211.

*Fransen, Piet. "The Authority of the Councils." In *Problems of Authority*, edited by John M. Todd, 43–78. Baltimore: Helicon, 1962.

————. *Hermeneutics of the Councils and Other Studies*. Collected by H. E. Mertens and F. De Graeve. Leuven: Leuven University and Uitgeverij Peeters, 1985.

Grillmeier, Alois. "Konzil und Rezeption." *Theologie und Philosophie* 45 (1970): 321–52.

————. "The Reception of Chalcedon in the Roman Catholic Church." *Ecumenical Review* 22 (1970): 383–411.

Hryniewicz, Waclaw. "Die ekklesiale Rezeption in der Sicht der orthodoxen Theologie." *Theologie und Glaube* 65 (1975): 250–66.

*Huizing, Peter, and Knut Walf, eds. *The Ecumenical Council: Its Significance in the Constitution of the Church*. Concilium, no. 167. New York: Seabury; Edinburgh: T & T Clark, 1983.

Küng, Hans. *The Council in Action*. New York: Sheed & Ward, 1963.

————. *Structures of the Church*. New York: T. Nelson, 1964. Paperback, Notre Dame, Ind.: University of Notre Dame, 1968.

Margull, Hans, ed., *The Councils of the Church*. Philadelphia: Fortress, 1966.

Müller, Hubert. "Rezeption und Konsens in der Kirche." *Österreichisches Archiv für Kirchenrecht* 27 (1976): 3–21.

Pagé, Roch. *The Diocesan Pastoral Council.* New York: Newman, 1970.

Peri, Vittorio. *I concili e le chiese: Ricerca storica sulla tradizione d'universalità dei sinodi ecumenici.* Rome: Studium, 1965.

Schwaiger, Georg. *Päpstlicher Primat und Autorität der allgemeinen Konzilien im Spiegel der Geschichte.* Paderborn: F. Schöningh, 1977.

Sieben, Hermann Josef. *Die Konzilsidee der Alten Kirche.* Paderborn: F. Schöningh, 1979. Three other volumes with the same publisher complete this work: Latin Middle Ages (1984), the Reformation through the eighteenth century (1988), and the nineteenth and twentieth centuries (1993).

United States Catholic Conference. *A National Pastoral Council: Pro and Con.* Washington, D.C.: USCC, 1971.

Vries, Wilhelm de. *Orient et occident: Les structures ecclésiales vues dans l'histoire des sept premiers conciles oecuméniques.* Paris: Cerf, 1971.

40

THE SYNOD OF BISHOPS AND THE EPISCOPAL CONFERENCE

Antón, Angel. *Conferencias episcopales ¿Instancias intermedias? El estado teológico de la cuestión.* Salamanca: Sígueme, 1989.

————. *Primado y colegialidad: Sus relaciones a la luz del primer Sínodo extraordinario.* Madrid: Católica, 1970.

Astorri, Romeo, ed. *Gli statuti delle conferenze episcopali.* Padua: Cedam, 1987. Vol. 1, *Europa.* Vol. 2, *America.* Edited by Ivan C. Ibán. 1989.

Bravi, Maurizio Claudio. *Il sinodo dei vescovi: Istituzione, fini e natura. Indagine teologico-giuridica.* Rome: Gregoriana, 1995.

*Caprile, Giovanni. *Il sinodo dei vescovi.* Rome: Civiltà cattolica, 1967–86. Nine volumes that examine in detail individual synods.

Las conferencias episcopales hoy. Actas del simposio de 1–3 Mayo, 1975. Salamanca: Universidad Pontificia, 1977.

Congar, Yves M.-J. "Synode épiscopal, primauté et collegialité épiscopale." In *Ministères et communion ecclésiale,* 187–227. Paris: Cerf, 1981.

Dvornik, Francis. "Origins of Episcopal Synods." In *The Once and*

Future Church, edited by James A. Coriden, 25–56. Staten Island, N.Y.: Alba House, 1971.

Fagiolo, Vincenzo. "Il synodus episcoporum: Origine, natura, struttura, compiti." In *La collegialità episcopale per il futuro della chiesa,* edited by Vincenzo Fagiola and Gino Concetti, 3–43. Florence: Vallecchi, 1969.

Feliciani, Giorgio. *Le conferenze episcopali.* Bologna: Il Mulino, 1974.

Fesquet, Henri. *Le synode et l'avenir de l'Église.* Paris: Centurion, 1972.

Green, James P. *Conferences of Bishops and the Exercise of the "Munus Docendi" of the Church.* Rome: P. Graziani, 1987.

Grootaers, Jan, and Joseph A. Selling. *The 1980 Synod of Bishops "On the Role of the Family": An Exposition of the Event and an Analysis of Its Texts.* Leuven: Leuven University and Uitgeverij Peeters, 1983.

Guillemette, François. *Théologie des conférences épiscopales: Une herméneutique de Vatican II.* Montreal: Médiaspaul, 1994.

John Paul II. *The Theological and Juridical Nature of Episcopal Conferences.* Apostolic Letter. *Origins* 28 (July 30, 1998): 152–58.

The Jurist 48/1 (1988). This entire issue presents the papers from a colloquium on the nature and future of episcopal conferences, which was held at Salamanca, Spain, January 3–8, 1988.

Laurentin, René. *Enjeu du deuxième synode et contestation dans l'Église.* Paris: Seuil, 1969.

——. *L'enjeu du synode, suite du concile.* Paris: Seuil, 1967.

——. *L'évangélisation après le IV synode.* Paris: Seuil, 1975.

——. *Le premier synode: Histoire et bilan.* Paris: Seuil, 1968.

————. *Réorientation de l'Église après le IIIe synode*. Paris: Seuil, 1972.

————. *Le synode permanent: Naissance et avenir*. Paris: Seuil, 1970.

Legrand, Hervé-M. "Synodes et conciles de l'après-concile: Quelques enjeux ecclésiologiques." *Nouvelle revue théologique* 98 (1976): 193–216.

Lettmann, Reinhard. "Episcopal Conferences in the New Canon Law." *Studia Canonica* 14 (1980): 347–67.

McManus, Frederick. "The Scope of Authority of Episcopal Conferences." In *The Once and Future Church*, edited by James A. Coriden, 129–78. Staten Island, N.Y.: Alba House, 1971.

Müller, Hubert, and Hermann J. Pottmeyer, eds. *Die Bischofskonferenz: Theologischer und juridischer Status*. Düsseldorf: Patmos, 1989. Articles by H. Müller, H. J. Pottmeyer, I. Fürer, H. J. Sieben, and others.

Murphy, Francis X., and Gary MacEoin. *Synod of '67: A New Sound in Rome*. Milwaukee, Wis.: Bruce, 1968.

Price, Bernard. "Episcopal Conferences and Collegiality." *Studia Canonica* 2 (1968): 125–32.

*Reese, Thomas J., ed. *Episcopal Conferences: Historical, Canonical, and Theological Studies*. Washington, D.C.: Georgetown University, 1989. Articles by T. J. Green, J. A. Komonchak, A. Dulles, and others.

Tomko, Josef, ed. *Il sinodo dei vescovi: Natura, metodo, prospettive*. Vatican City: Libreria Editrice Vaticana, 1985.

41

THE PARTICULAR OR LOCAL CHURCH

Contri, Antonio. "La teologia della chiesa locale e i suoi orienta-
menti fondamentali." *Euentes Docete* 25 (1972): 331–401.
Annotated bibliography on the local church.

Mariotti, Mario. "Appunti bibliografici." *Vita e Pensiero* 54
(1971): 347–75. Annotated bibliography on the local
church.

• • •

Allmen, Jean Jacques von. "L'Église locale parmi les autres
églises locales." *Irénikon* 43 (1970): 512–37.

Amato, Angelo, ed., *La chiesa locale*. Rome: Libreria Ateneo Sale-
siano, 1976.

Bazatole, B. "L'évêque et la vie chrétienne au sein de l'Église
locale." In *L'épiscopat et l'Église universelle,* edited by Y. J.-M.
Congar and B.-D. Dupuy, 329–60. Paris: Cerf, 1962.

Beinert, Wolfgang. "Dogmenhistorische Anmerkungen zum
Begriff 'Partikularkirche'." *Theologie und Philosophie* 50
(1975): 38–69.

———. "Die Kirche Christi als Lokalkirche." *Una Sancta* 32
(1977): 114–29.

Curran, Charles E., and George J. Dyer, eds. *Shared Responsibility in the Local Church*. Chicago: Chicago Studies, 1970.

Dortel-Claudot, Michel. *Églises locales–Église universelle: Comment se gouverne le peuple de Dieu*. Lyon: Le Chalet, 1973.

Ernst, Josef. "From the Local Community to the Great Church. Illustrated from the Church Patterns of Philippians and Ephesians." *Biblical Theology Bulletin* 6 (1976): 237–57.

*Granfield, Patrick. "The Church Local and Universal: Realization of Communion." *The Jurist* 49 (1989): 449–71.

Joint Working Group (Roman Catholic Church and The World Council of Churches). *The Notion of "Hierarchy of Truths" and the Church: Local and Universal*. Faith and Order Paper no. 150. Geneva: World Council of Churches, 1990.

The Jurist 52/1 (1992). This entire issue presents the papers from a colloquium on the local church and catholicity, which was held at Salamanca, Spain, April 2–7, 1991.

Komonchak, Joseph A. "The Church Universal as the Communion of Local Churches." In *Where Does the Church Stand?*, edited by Giuseppe Alberigo, 30–35. Concilium, no. 146. Edinburgh: T & T Clark, 1981.

Lanne, Emmanuel. "The Local Church: Its Catholicity and Its Apostolicity." *One in Christ* 6 (1970): 288–313.

Legrand, Hervé-M. "La réalisation de l'Église en un lieu." In *Initiation à la pratique de la théologie*, edited by B. Lauret and F. Refoulé, 3:143–345. Paris: Cerf, 1983.

———. "The Revaluation of Local Churches: Some Theological Implications." In *The Unifying Role of the Bishop*, edited by Edward Schillebeeckx, 53–64. Concilium, no. 71. New York: Herder and Herder, 1972.

López-Illana, Francesco. *Ecclesia unum et plura: Riflessione teologico-canonica sull'autonomia della Chiese locali*. Vatican City: Libreria Editrice Vaticana, 1991.

*Lubac, Henri de. *The Motherhood of the Church, followed by Particular Churches in the Universal Church*. San Francisco: Ignatius, 1982.

Morgante, Marcello. *La chiesa particolare nel Codice di Diritto Canonico*. Milan: Paoline, 1987.

Neunheuser, Burkhard. "Église universelle et Église locale." In *L'Église de Vatican II,* edited by G. Baraúna, 2:607–38. Unam Sanctam, no. 51b. Paris: Cerf, 1966. Italian version: *La Chiesa del Vaticano II*. Florence: Vallecchi, 1965. German version: *De Ecclesia: Beiträge zur Konstitution über die Kirche des II. Vatikanischen Konzils*. Freiburg: Herder, 1966.

O'Rourke, John J. "The Office of Bishop and its Relationship to the Particular Churches and to the United States." *Studia Canonica* 5 (1971): 227–44.

Pagé, Roch. *Les Églises particulières*. 2 vols. Montreal: Paulines, 1985, 1989.

Proceedings of the Catholic Theological Society of America 35 (1980). Articles on local church by P. Granfield, S. Kilian, F. Parrella, and B. Prusak.

Proceedings of the Catholic Theological Society of America 36 (1981). Articles on local church by R. E. Brown, M. Fahey, J. Komonchak, and others.

Rodriguez, Pedro. *Particular Churches and Personal Prelatures*. Dublin: Four Courts, 1986.

Tessarolo, Andrea, ed. *La chiesa locale*. Bologna: Dehoniane, 1970.

*Tillard, Jean-Marie R. *L'Église locale: Ecclésiologie de communion et catholicité*. Paris: Cerf, 1995.

Villar, José R. *Teología de la Iglesia particular: El tema en la literatura de lengua francesa hasta el Concilio Vaticano II*. Pamplona: Universidad de Navarra, 1989.

World Council of Churches. *In Each Place: Towards a Fellowship of Local Churches Truly United.* Geneva: WCC, 1977.

Zbignievus, Joseph T. *Actualisatio ecclesiae universalis in ecclesia locali iuxta Concilii Vaticani II.* Rome: Angelicum, 1970.

THE PARISH

The following authors apply the theology of the local church to the parish.

Arnold, Franz Xaver, et al. *Handbuch der Pastoraltheologie*, 3:111–262. Freiburg: Herder, 1968. Articles by N. Greinacher, A. Müller, R. Fischer-Wollpert, and others.

Bausch, William J. *The Parish of the Next Millennium*. Mystic, Conn.: Twenty-Third, 1997.

Bishops Committee on Priestly Life and Ministry. *A Shepherd's Care: Reflections on the Changing Role of a Pastor*. Washington, D.C.: USCC, 1987.

*Blöchlinger, Alex. *The Modern Parish Community*. New York: P. J. Kenedy, 1965.

Bordelon, Marvin, ed. *The Parish in a Time of Change*. Notre Dame, Ind.: Fides, 1967.

Brennan, Patrick J. *The Evangelizing Parish: Theologies and Strategies for Renewal*. Allen, Tex., and Valencia, Calif.: Tabor, 1987.

———. *Re-Imagining Evangelization: Toward the Reign of God and the Communal Parish*. New York: Crossroad, 1995.

———. *Re-Imagining the Parish*. New York: Crossroad, 1990.

Connan, Francis, and Jean Claude Barreau. *Demain, la paroisse.* Paris: Seuil, 1966.

*Coriden, James A. *The Parish in Catholic Tradition: History, Theology, and Canon Law.* New York and Mahwah, N.J.: Paulist, 1997.

Cusack, Barbara Anne, and Teresa Sullivan. *Pastoral Care in Parishes Without Pastors.* Washington, D.C.: Canon Law Society of America, 1995.

Davis, Charles. "The Parish and Theology." *Clergy Review* 49 (1964): 265–90.

DeSiano, Frank, and Kenneth Boyack. *Creating the Evangelizing Parish.* New York and Mahwah, N.J.: Paulist, 1995.

Dolan, Jay P. *The American Catholic Parish: A History from 1850 to the Present.* 2 vols. New York: Paulist, 1987.

Dolan, Jay P., R. Scott Appleby, Patricia Byrne, and Debra Campbell. *Transforming Parish Ministry: The Changing Roles of Catholic Clergy, Laity, and Women Religious.* New York: Crossroad, 1989.

Downs, Thomas. *The Parish as Learning Community.* New York: Paulist, 1979.

Floristan, Casiano. *The Parish–Eucharistic Community.* Notre Dame, Ind.: Fides, 1964.

Foley, Gerald. *Family-Centered Church: A New Parish Model.* Kansas City, Mo.: Sheed & Ward, 1995.

Geaney, Dennis J. *The Prophetic Parish: A Center for Peace and Justice.* Minneapolis: Winston, 1983.

Greeley, Andrew M., et al. *Parish, Priest, and People.* Chicago: Thomas More, 1981.

Gremillion, Joseph, and Jim Castelli. *The Emerging Parish: The Notre Dame Study of Catholic Life Since Vatican II*. San Francisco: Harper & Row, 1987.

*Kilian, Sabbas J. *Theological Models for the Parish*. Staten Island, N.Y.: Alba House, 1977.

Michonneau, Georges. *Revolution in a City Parish*. Westminster, Md.: Newman, 1949.

National Conference of Catholic Bishops. "Communities of Salt and Light: Reflections on Parish Social Mission." *Origins* 23 (Dec. 2, 1993): 443–48.

———. *The Parish: A People, A Mission, A Structure*. Washington, D.C.: USCC, 1980.

———. *Parish Life in the United States: Final Report to the Bishops of United States by the Parish Project*. Washington, D.C.: USCC, 1983.

Newsome, Robert R. *The Ministering Parish: Methods and Procedures for the Pastoral Organization*. New York: Paulist, 1982.

O'Gara, James, ed. *The Postconciliar Parish*. New York: P. J. Kenedy, 1967.

Quinn, Bernard. *The Small Rural Parish*. Washington, D.C.: Glenmary Research Center, 1980.

Rademacher, William J. *The Practical Guide for Parish Councils*. Mystic, Conn.: Twenty-Third, 1980.

*Rahner, Hugo, ed. *The Parish from Theology to Practice*. Westminster, Md.: Newman, 1958.

Roy, Paul S. *Building Christian Communities for Justice*. New York: Paulist, 1981.

Searle, Mark, ed. *Parish: A Place for Worship*. Collegeville, Minn.: Liturgical Press, 1981.

Sweetser, Thomas. *Successful Parishes: How They Meet the Challenge of Peace*. Minneapolis: Winston, 1983.

Sweetser, Thomas, and Patricia Forster. *Transforming the Parish: Models for the Future*. Kansas City, Mo.: Sheed & Ward, 1993.

Sweetser, Thomas, and Carol M. Holden. *Leadership in a Successful Parish*. San Francisco: Harper & Row, 1987.

Wallace, Ruth A. *They Call Her Pastor: A New Role for Catholic Women*. Albany: State University of New York, 1992.

Whitehead, Evelyn E., ed. *The Parish in Community and Ministry*. New York: Paulist, 1978.

Whitehead, Evelyn E., and James D. Whitehead. *Community of Faith: Models and Strategies for Developing Christian Communities*. New York: Seabury, 1973.

43

CHARISMS IN THE CHURCH

Burgess, Stanley M., ed. *Dictionary of Pentecostal and Charismatic Movements*. Grand Rapids, Mich.: Zondervan, 1988.

• • •

Agrimson, J. Elmo, ed. *Gifts of the Spirit and the Body of Christ: Perspectives on the Charismatic Movement*. Minneapolis: Augsburg, 1974.

*Congar, Yves M.-J. *I Believe in the Holy Spirit*, 2:147–201. New York: Seabury, 1983.

Culpepper, Robert H. *Evaluating the Charismatic Movement: A Theological and Biblical Appraisal*. Valley Forge, Pa.: Judson, 1977.

Duquoc, Christian, and Casiano Floristan, eds. *Charisms in the Church*. Concilium, no. 109. New York: Seabury, 1978.

Fichter, Joseph. *The Catholic Cult of the Paraclete*. New York: Sheed & Ward, 1975.

Gelpi, Donald. *Charism and Sacrament: A Theology of Christian Conversion*. New York: Paulist, 1976.

Hasenhüttl, Gotthold. *Charisma: Ordnungsprinzip der Kirche*. Freiburg: Herder, 1969.

Hollenweger, Walter J. *The Pentecostals: The Charismatic Movement in the Churches.* Minneapolis: Augsburg, 1972.

Jones, J. *Filled with New Wine: The Charismatic Renewal of the Church.* New York: Harper & Row, 1976.

Küng, Hans. "The Charismatic Structure of the Church." In *Pastoral Reform in Church Government,* edited by Neophytos Edelby and Teodoro Jiménez-Urresti, 41–61. Concilium, no. 8. Glen Rock, N.J.: Paulist, 1965.

Martin, David, and Peter Mullen, eds. *Strange Gifts? A Guide to Charismatic Renewal.* New York: Blackwell, 1985.

McDonnell, Kilian. *The Charismatic Renewal and Ecumenism.* New York: Paulist, 1978.

———. *Charismatic Renewal and the Churches.* New York: Seabury, 1976.

———, ed. *The Holy Spirit and Power.* Garden City, N.Y.: Doubleday, 1975.

———, ed. *Presence, Power, Praise: Documents on the Charismatic Renewal.* 3 vols. Collegeville, Minn.: Liturgical Press, 1980.

McDonnell, Kilian, and George T. Montague. *Christian Initiation and Baptism in the Holy Spirit: Evidence from the First Eight Centuries.* Rev. ed. Collegeville, Minn.: Liturgical Press, 1994.

Mühlen, Heribert. *A Charismatic Theology: Initiation in the Spirit.* New York: Paulist, 1978.

Quebedeaux, Richard. *The New Charismatics II.* San Francisco: Harper & Row, 1983.

*Rahner, Karl. *The Dynamic Element in the Church.* New York: Herder and Herder, 1964.

Schürmann, Heinz. "Les charismes spirituels." In *L'Église de Vatican II,* edited by G. Baraúna, 2:541–73. 3 vols. Unam Sanctam, no. 51 a, b, c. Paris: Cerf, 1966. Italian version: *La Chiesa del Vaticano II*. Florence: Vallecchi, 1965. German version: *De Ecclesia: Beiträge zur Konstitution über die Kirche des II. Vatikanischen Konzils*. Freiburg: Herder, 1966.

Suenens, Léon Joseph. *A New Pentecost?* New York: Seabury, 1975.

*Sullivan, Francis A. *Charisms and Charismatic Renewal: A Biblical and Theological Study*. Ann Arbor, Mich.: Servant, 1982.

Theological and Pastoral Orientations on the Charismatic Renewal. Prepared at Malines, Belgium. Notre Dame, Ind.: Communication Center, 1974.

44

ORDAINED MINISTERS IN THE CHURCH

A. The Priesthood

Balthasar, Hans Urs von. "Office in the Church." In *Spouse of the Word: Explorations in Theology*, 2:81–141. San Francisco: Ignatius, 1991.

Bartlett, David L. *Ministry in the New Testament*. Minneapolis: Fortress, 1993.

Bernier, Paul. *Ministry in the Church: A Historical and Pastoral Approach*. Mystic, Conn.: Twenty-Third, 1992.

Brown, Raymond E. *Priest and Bishop: Biblical Reflections*. New York: Paulist, 1970.

Burrows, William R. *New Ministries: The Global Context*. Maryknoll, N.Y.: Orbis, 1980.

*Congar, Yves M.-J. *Ministères et communion ecclésiale*. Paris: Cerf, 1971.

Cooke, Bernard. *Ministry to Word and Sacraments*. Philadelphia: Fortress, 1976.

Cordes, Paul J. *Sendung zum Dienst: Exegetisch-historische und systematische Studien zum Konzilsdekret "vom Dienst und Leben der Priester."* Frankfurt: J. Knecht, 1972.

Cowan, Michael A., ed. *Leadership Ministry in Community.* Vol. 6 of *Alternative Futures for Worship.* Collegeville, Minn.: Liturgical Press, 1987. Articles by D. N. Power, E. E. Whitehead, J. D. Whitehead, and J. Shea.

Dallen, James. *The Dilemma of Priestless Sundays.* Chicago: Liturgy Training Publications, 1994.

Delorme, Jean. *Le ministère et les ministères selon le Nouveau Testament.* Paris: Seuil, 1974.

Dinter, Paul E. *The Changing Priesthood: From the Bible to the 21st Century.* Chicago: Thomas More, 1996.

Donovan, Daniel. *What Are They Saying about the Ministerial Priesthood?* New York: Paulist, 1992.

Drilling, Peter. *Trinity and Ministry.* Minneapolis: Augsburg Fortress, 1991.

*Dulles, Avery. *The Priestly Office: A Theological Reflection.* New York and Mahwah, N.J.: Paulist, 1997.

Farmer, Jerry T. *Ministry in Community: Rahner's Vision of Ministry.* Louvain: Peeters; Grand Rapids, Mich.: Wm. B. Eerdmans, 1993.

*Galot, Jean. *Theology of the Priesthood.* San Francisco: Ignatius, 1984.

Grollenberg, Lucas, et al. *Minister? Pastor? Prophet? Grassroots Leadership in the Church.* New York: Crossroad, 1981. Articles by J. Kerkhofs, A. Houtepen, J. J. A. Vollebergh, and E. Schillebeeckx.

Hastings, Adrian. *Church and Ministry.* Kampala: Gaba, 1972.

Hennessy, Paul K., ed. *A Concert of Charisms: Ordained Ministry in Religious Life.* New York and Mahwah, N.J.: Paulist, 1997.

Hill, Edmund. *Ministry and Authority in the Catholic Church*. London: Geoffrey Chapman, 1988.

Hoge, Dean R. *The Future of Catholic Leadership: Responses to the Priest Shortage*. Kansas City, Mo.: Sheed & Ward, 1987.

Iersel, Bas van, and Roland Murphy, eds. *Office and Ministry in the Church*. Concilium, no. 80. New York: Herder and Herder, 1972.

John Paul II. "*Pastores Dabo Vobis:* A Post-Synodal Apostolic Exhortation on the Formation of Priests in the Circumstances of the Present Day." *Origins* 21(April 16, 1992): 717, 719–59.

Lawler, Michael G. *A Theology of Ministry*. Kansas City, Mo.: Sheed & Ward, 1990.

Lécuyer, Joseph, et al. "Decree on the Ministry and Life of Priests." In *Commentary on the Documents of Vatican II*, edited by Herbert Vorgrimler, 4:183–297. New York: Herder and Herder, 1969.

Lemaire, André. *Les ministères aux origines de l'Église: Naissance de la triple hierarchie: Évêques, presbytres, diacres*. Paris: Cerf, 1971.

Lienhard, Joseph T. *Ministry*. Wilmington, Del.: Michael Glazier, 1984. A selection of patristic texts.

Macquarrie, John. *Theology, Church, and Ministry*. New York: Crossroad, 1986.

McBrien, Richard P. *Ministry: A Theological-Pastoral Handbook*. San Francisco: Harper & Row, 1987.

Mitchell, Nathan. *Mission and Ministry: History and Theology in the Sacrament of Order*. Wilmington, Del.: Michael Glazier, 1982.

Mohler, James A. *The Origin and Evolution of the Priesthood*. Staten Island, N.Y.: Alba House, 1970.

Neuhaus, Richard John. *Freedom for Ministry: A Critical Affirmation of the Church and its Mission*. San Francisco and London: Harper & Row, 1979. Rev. ed. Grand Rapids, Mich.: Wm. B. Eerdmans, 1992.

Nichols, Aidan. *Holy Order: Apostolic Priesthood from the New Testament to the Second Vatican Council*. Dublin: Veritas, 1990.

Niebuhr, H. Richard. *The Purpose of the Church and its Ministry*. New York: Harper, 1956.

O'Grady, John F. *Disciples and Leaders: The Origins of Christian Ministry in the New Testament*. New York and Mahwah, N.J.: Paulist, 1991.

O'Meara, Thomas F. *Theology of Ministry*. New York: Paulist, 1983, 1999.

*Osborne, Kenan B. *Priesthood: A History of Ordained Ministry in the Roman Catholic Church*. New York: Paulist, 1989.

Perri, William D. *A Radical Challenge for Priesthood Today: From Trial to Transformation*. Mystic, Conn.: Twenty-Third, 1996.

Poling, James N., and Donald E. Miller. *Foundations for a Practical Theology of Ministry*. Nashville, Tenn.: Abingdon, 1985.

Power, David N. *The Christian Priest: Elder and Prophet*. London: Sheed & Ward, 1973.

———. *Ministers of Christ and His Church. The Theology of Priesthood*. London: Geoffrey Chapman, 1969.

Provost, James H., ed. *Official Ministry in a New Age*. Washington, D.C.: Canon Law Society of America, 1981. Articles by J. H. Provost, C. Osiek, J. Komonchak, and others.

Schillebeeckx, Edward. "The Catholic Understanding of Office in the Church." *Theological Studies* 30 (1969): 567–87. Reprinted in his *Mission of the Church*, 205–28. New York: Seabury, 1973.

————. *The Church with A Human Face: A New and Expanded Theology of Ministry*. New York: Crossroad, 1985.

————. *Ministry: Leadership in the Community of Jesus*. New York: Crossroad, 1981.

Schner, George P. *Education for Ministry: Reform and Renewal in Theological Education*. Kansas City, Mo.: Sheed & Ward, 1993.

Schoenherr, Richard A., Lawrence A. Young, with collaboration of Tsan-Yuang Cheng. *Full Pews and Empty Altars*. Madison, Wis.: University of Wisconsin, 1993.

Stone, Bryan P. *Compassionate Ministry: Theological Foundations*. Maryknoll, N.Y.: Orbis, 1996.

Tavard, George H. *A Theology for Ministry*. Wilmington, Del.: Michael Glazier, 1983.

Vilela, Albano. *La condition collégiale des prêtres du IIIe siècle*. Paris: Beauchesne, 1971.

Wasselynck, René. *Les prêtres: Elaboration du décret Presbyterorum ordinis de Vatican II*. Paris: Desclée, 1968.

Whitehead, Evelyn Eaton, and James D. Whitehead. *Method in Ministry*. New York: Seabury, 1981.

B. The Diaconate

Canon Law Society of America, Ad Hoc Committee. *The Canonical Implications of Ordaining Women to the Permanent Diaconate*. Washington, D.C.: Canon Law Society of America, 1995.

Congregation for Catholic Education. "Basic Norms for the Formation of Permanent Deacons." Congregation for the Clergy. "Directory for the Ministry and Life of Permanent Deacons." *Origins* 28 (August 27, 1998): 177, 179–204.

Martimort, Aimé-Georges. *Deaconesses: An Historical Study*. San Francisco: Ignatius, 1986.

*McCaslin, Patrick, and Michael G. Lawler. *Sacrament of Service: A Vision of the Permanent Diaconate Today*. New York and Mahwah, N.J.: Paulist, 1986.

National Conference of Catholic Bishops. *Foundations for the Renewal of the Diaconate*. Washington, D.C.: USCC, 1993.

*————. *A National Study on the Permanent Diaconate of the Catholic Church of the United States: 1994–1995*. Washington, D.C.: USCC, 1996.

————. *Permanent Deacons in the United States: Guidelines on their Formation and Ministry*. Washington, D.C.: USCC, 1985.

Nowell, Robert. *The Ministry of Service: Deacons in the Contemporary Church*. New York: Herder and Herder, 1968.

Plater, Ormonde. *Many Servants: An Introduction to Deacons*. Boston: Cowley, 1991. A study of deacons in the Episcopal Church.

Sherman, Lynn C. *The Deacon in the Church*. Staten Island, N.Y.: Alba House, 1991.

Shugrue, Timothy J. *Service Ministry of the Deacon*. Washington, D.C.: NCCB, 1988.

Winninger, Paul. *Diacres: Histoire et avenir du diaconat*. Paris: Centurion, 1967.

Winninger, Paul, and Yves M.-J. Congar, eds. *Le diacre dans l'Église et le monde d'aujourd'hui*. Unam Sanctam, no. 59. Paris: Cerf, 1966.

45

RELIGIOUS IN THE CHURCH

Pellicia, Guerrino, and Giancarlo Rocca, eds. *Dizionario degli istituti di perfezione*. Rome: Paoline, 1974–. A continuing multivolume work.

• • •

*Arbuckle, Gerald A. *Out of Chaos: Refounding Religious Congregations*. New York: Paulist, 1988.

*Azevedo, Marcello. *Vocation for Mission: The Challenge of Religious Life Today*. New York: Paulist, 1988.

Balthasar, Hans Urs von. *The Christian State of Life*. San Francisco: Ignatius, 1983.

Beyer, Jean. *Religious Life or Secular Institute?* Rome: Gregoriana, 1970.

*Cada, Lawrence, et al. *Shaping of the Coming Age of Religious Life*. New York: Seabury, 1979.

Clarke, Thomas E. *New Pentecost or New Passion? The Directions of Religious Life Today*. New York: Paulist, 1973.

Congregation for Institutes of Consecrated Life and Societies of Apostolic Life. "Fraternal Life in Community." *Origins* 23 (March 24, 1994): 693, 695–712.

Cussiánovich, Alejandro. *Religious Life and the Poor: Liberation Theology Perspective.* Maryknoll, N.Y.: Orbis, 1979.

Daly, Robert J., et al. *Religious Life in the U.S. Church: The New Dialogue.* New York: Paulist, 1984. Articles by J. R. Quinn, J. Hennesey, J. W. Padberg, E. McDonough, and others.

Dyer, Ralph J. *The New Religious: An Authentic Life.* Milwaukee, Wis.: Bruce, 1971.

Gelpi, Donald L. *Discerning the Spirit: Foundations and Futures of Religious Life.* New York: Sheed & Ward, 1970.

Huizing, Peter, and William Bassett, eds. *The Future of Religious Life.* Concilium, no. 97. New York: Herder and Herder, 1974–75.

Huyghe, Gérard, et al. *Religious Orders in the Modern World.* Westminster, Md.: Newman, 1965. Articles by K. Rahner, J. Hamer, J. Urtasun, and others.

John Paul II. "*Vita Consecrata*: A Post-Synodal Apostolic Exhortation on the Consecrated Life." *Origins* 25 (April 4, 1996): 681, 683–719.

Kline, Francis. *Lovers of the Place: Monasticism Loose in the Church.* Collegeville, Minn.: Liturgical Press, 1997.

Kolbenschlag, Madonna, ed. *Between God and Caesar: Priests, Sisters, and Political Office in the United States.* Maryknoll, N.Y.: Orbis, 1985.

Kolmer, Elizabeth. *Religious Women in the United States: A Survey of the Influential Literature from 1950 to 1983.* Wilmington, Del.: Michael Glazier, 1984.

Lozano, John M. *Discipleship: Toward an Understanding of Religious Life.* 2nd ed. Chicago: Claret Center for Resources in Spirituality, 1983.

Martelet, Gustave. *The Church's Holiness and Religious Life.* St. Marys, Kan.: Review for Religious, 1966.

McNamara, Jo Ann Kay. *Sisters in Arms: Catholic Nuns Through Two Millennia*. Cambridge, Mass.: Harvard University, 1996.

Moloney, Francis. *A Life of Promise: Poverty, Chastity, Obedience*. Wilmington, Del.: Michael Glazier, 1984.

Moran, Gabriel, and Maria Harris. *Experiences in Community: Should Religious Life Survive?* New York: Herder and Herder, 1968.

Neal, Marie Augusta. *Catholic Sisters in Transition: From the 1960's to the 1980's*. Wilmington, Del.: Michael Glazier, 1984.

O'Murchu, Diarmuid. *Religious Life: A Prophetic Vision*. Notre Dame, Ind.: Ave Maria, 1991.

Orsy, Ladislas M. *Open to the Spirit: Religious Life after Vatican II*. Washington, D.C.: Corpus, 1968.

Tillard, Jean M. R. *Devant Dieu et pour le monde: Le projet des religieux*. Paris: Desclée De Brouwer, 1966.

Tillard, J. M. R., and Yves M.-J. Congar, eds. *L'adaptation et la rénovation de la vie religieuse: Décret "Perfectae caritatis."* Unam Sanctam, no. 62. Paris: Cerf, 1967.

Wulf, Friedrich. "Decree on the Appropriate Renewal of the Religious Life." In *Commentary on the Documents of Vatican II*, edited by Herbert Vorgrimler, 2:301–70. New York: Herder and Herder, 1968.

Yuhaus, Cassian J., ed. *Religious Life: The Challenge for Tomorrow*. New York and Mahwah, N.J.: Paulist, 1994.

46

LAITY IN THE CHURCH

Doohan, Leonard. *The Laity: A Bibliography*. Wilmington, Del.: Michael Glazier, 1987.

Goldie, Rosemary. "Lay, Laity, Laicity: A Bibliographical Survey of Three Decades. Elements for a Theology of the Laity." *The Laity Today* 26 (1979): 107–43. Vatican City: Vatican Press, 1979.

International Congress on the Lay Apostolate. *L'apostolato dei laici: Bibliografia sistematica*. Milan: Vita e Pensiero, 1957. Bibliography on the laity from 1922 to 1957.

· · ·

Barta, Russell, ed. *Challenge to the Laity*. Huntington, Ind.: Our Sunday Visitor, 1980. Contains the text of the Chicago Declaration of Christian Concern and articles by E. Marciniak, M. Novak, J. Coleman, and S. Shriver.

Boff, Leonardo. *God's Witnesses in the Heart of the World*. Chicago: Claret Center for Resources in Spirituality, 1981.

Collins, Mary, and David Power, eds. *Can We Always Celebrate the Eucharist?* Concilium, no. 152. New York: Seabury; Edinburgh: T & T Clark, 1982.

Congar, Yves M.-J. *Laity, Church, and World*. Baltimore: Helicon, 1960.

*————. *Lay People in the Church*. Westminster, Md.: Newman, 1957.

————. *Ministères et communion ecclésiale*. Paris: Cerf, 1971. Chapter 1 is also in English: "My Pathfindings in the Theology of the Laity." *The Jurist* 32 (1972): 169–88.

Congregation for the Clergy, et al. Instruction: "Some Questions Regarding 'Collaboration of Nonordained Faithful in Priests' Sacred Ministry." *Origins* 27 (Nov. 27, 1997): 397, 399–410.

Dabin, Paul. *Le sacerdoce royal des fidèles dans la tradition ancienne et moderne*. Brussels: Desclée De Brouwer, 1950.

————. *Le sacerdoce royal des fidèles dans les livres saints*. Paris: Bloud, 1941.

*D'Antonio, William V., James D. Davidson, Dean R. Hoge, and Ruth A. Wallace. *Laity: American and Catholic: Transforming the Church*. Kansas City, Mo.: Sheed & Ward, 1996.

Doohan, Leonard. *Laity's Mission in the Local Church: Setting a New Direction*. San Francisco: Harper & Row, 1986.

————. *The Lay-Centered Church: Theology and Spirituality*. Minneapolis: Winston, 1984.

Droel, William L., and Gregory Pierce. *Confident and Competent: A Challenge for the Lay Church*. Notre Dame, Ind.: Ave Maria, 1987.

Faivre, Alexandre. *The Emergence of the Laity in the Early Church*. New York and Mahwah, N.J.: Paulist, 1990.

Fenhagen, James. *Mutual Ministry*. New York: Seabury, 1977.

Flood, Edmund. *The Laity Today and Tomorrow: A Report on the New Consciousness of Lay Catholics*. Mahwah, N.J.: Paulist, 1987.

Foley, Gerald. *Empowering the Laity.* Kansas City, Mo.: Sheed & Ward, 1986.

Fox, Zeni. *New Eccesial Ministry: Lay Professionals Serving the Church.* Kansas City, Mo.: Sheed & Ward, 1997.

Gregorianum 68:1–2 (1987). Issue devoted entirely to the theology of lay people in the church. Articles by U. Vanni, J. Beyer, J. Dupuis, and others.

Grootaers, Jan. *Le chantier reste ouvert: Les laïcs dans l'Eglise et dans le monde.* Paris: Centurion, 1988.

John Paul II. *Christifideles Laici.* Apostolic Exhortation on the Laity. *Origins* 18 (Feb. 9, 1989): 561, 563–95.

Kinast, Robert L. *Caring for Society: A Theological Interpretation of Lay Ministry.* Chicago: Thomas More, 1985.

Klostermann, Ferdinand. "Der Apostolat der Laier in der Kirche." In *Handbuch der Pastoraltheologie,* edited by Franz Xaver Arnold et al., 3:586–635. Freiburg: Herder, 1968.

*————. "Decree on the Apostolate of the Laity." In *Commentary on the Documents of Vatican II,* edited by Herbert Vorgrimler, 3:273–404. New York: Herder and Herder, 1969. See also 1:231–52.

Leckey, Dolores R. *Laity Stirring the Church: Prophetic Questions.* Philadelphia: Fortress, 1987.

Lennan, Richard, ed. *Redefining the Church: Vision and Practice.* Alexandria, Australia: E. J. Dwyer, 1995.

National Conference of Catholic Bishops. *Called and Gifted.* Washington, D.C.: USCC, 1980.

————. *To Build and Be Church.* Washington, D.C.: USCC, 1979.

O'Gara, James, ed. *The Layman in the Church.* New York: Herder and Herder, 1962. Articles by J. T. Ellis, R. W. Hovda, J. G. Lawler, and others.

Oliver, Robert W. *The Vocation of the Laity to Evangelize.* Rome: Gregoriana, 1997.

*Osborne, Kenan. *Ministry: Lay Ministry in the Roman Catholic Church.* New York and Mahwah, N.J.: Paulist, 1993.

Parent, Rémi. *A Church of the Baptized: Overcoming the Tension between the Clergy and the Laity.* New York and Mahwah, N.J.: Paulist, 1989.

Peck, George, and John S. Hoffman, eds. *The Laity in Ministry: The Whole People of God for the Whole World.* Valley Forge, Pa.: Judson, 1984.

Pellitero, Ramiro. *La teología de laicado en la obra de Yves Congar.* Pamplona: Universidad de Navarra, 1996.

Philips, Gérard. *Achieving Christian Maturity.* Chicago: Franciscan Herald, 1966.

———. *The Role of the Laity in the Church.* Chicago: Fides, 1956.

Portillo, Alvaro Del. *Faithful and Laity in the Church.* Shannon: Ecclesia, 1972.

Power, David N. *Gifts that Differ: Lay Ministries Established and Unestablished.* New York: Pueblo, 1980.

Pro Mundi Vita Bulletin, No. 50, 1974. New Forms of Ministry in Christian Communities.

Rademacher, William J. *Lay Ministry: A Theological, Spiritual, and Pastoral Handbook.* New York: Crossroad, 1991.

Rahner, Karl. "Notes on the Lay Apostolate." In *Theological Investigations,* 2:219–352. New York: Crossroad, 1963. See also other articles on the laity in vols. 3 and 8 of *Theological Investigations.*

Schillebeeckx, Edward. "The Typological Definition of the Christian Laymen according to Vatican II." In his *The Mission of the Church,* 90–117. New York: Seabury, 1973.

Sesboüé, Bernard. *N'ayez pas peur: Regards sur l'Église et ses ministères aujourd'hui*. Paris: Desclée De Brouwer, 1996.

Shaw, Russell. *To Hunt, To Shoot, To Entertain: Clericalism and the Catholic Laity*. San Francisco: Ignatius, 1993.

Thils, Gustave. *Les laïcs et l'enjeu des temps "post-modernes."* Louvain: Faculté de Théologie, 1988.

Whitehead, James, and Evelyn Eaton Whitehead. *The Emerging Laity: Returning Leadership to the Community of Faith*. Garden City, N.Y.: Doubleday, 1986.

47

WOMEN IN THE CHURCH

Finson, Shelley Davis. *Women and Religion: A Bibliographic Guide to Christian Feminist Liberation Theology*. Toronto: University of Toronto, 1991.

• • •

Aquino, María Pillar. *Our Cry for Life: Feminist Theology from Latin America*. Maryknoll, N.Y.: Orbis, 1993.

Ashe, Kaye. *The Feminization of the Church*. Kansas City, Mo.: Sheed & Ward, 1997.

Ashley, Benedict M. *Justice in the Church: Gender and Participation*. Washington, D.C.: Catholic University of America, 1996.

Bouyer, Louis. *Woman in the Church*. San Francisco: Ignatius, 1979.

Butler, Sara, ed. *Research Report: Women in Church and Society*. Mahwah, N.J.: Catholic Theological Society of America, 1978.

Carr, Anne E. *Transforming Grace: Christian Tradition and Women's Experience*. New York: Continuum, 1996.

Chittister, Joan. *Women, Ministry, and the Church*. New York: Paulist, 1983.

Clark, Elizabeth A. *Women in the Early Church*. Wilmington, Del.: Michael Glazier, 1983.

Congregazione per la Dottrina della Fede. *Dall' "Inter Insigniores" all' "Ordinatio Sacerdotalis." Documenti e commenti*. Vatican City: Libreria Editrice Vaticana, 1996.

Elizondo, Virgil, and Norbert Greinacher, eds. *Women in a Man's Church*. Concilium, no. 134. New York: Seabury, 1980.

Ermath, Margaret Sittler. *Adam's Fractured Rib: Observations on Women in the Church*. Philadelphia: Fortress, 1970.

Fiorenza, Elisabeth Schüssler. *Discipleship of Equals: A Critical Feminist Ekklesia-logy of Liberation*. New York: Crossroad, 1993.

————. *In Memory of Her: A Feminist Theological Reconstruction of Christian Origins*. New York: Crossroad, 1983.

Galot, Jean. *L'Église et la femme*. Gembloux: J. Duculot, 1965.

Gryson, Roger. *Ministry of Women in the Early Church*. Collegeville, Minn.: Liturgical Press, 1976.

Harkness, Georgia Elma. *Women in Church und Society: A Historical and Theological Inquiry*. Nashville, Tenn.: Abingdon, 1972.

Kolbenschlag, Madonna, ed. *Women in the Church I*. Washington, D.C.: Pastoral, 1987.

Laflaive, Anne. *La femme et l'Église*. Paris: France-Empire, 1968.

*Martin, Francis. *The Feminist Question: Feminist Theology in the Light of Christian Tradition*. Grand Rapids, Mich.: Wm. B. Eerdmans, 1994.

Moltmann-Wendel, Elizabeth. *Liberty, Equality, Sisterhood: On the Emancipation of Women in Church and Society*. Philadelphia: Fortress, 1978.

*Osiek, Carolyn. *Beyond Anger: On Being a Feminist in the Church.* New York and Mahwah, N.J.: Paulist, 1986.

Ruether, Rosemary Radford, ed. *Religion and Sexism: Images of Women in the Jewish and Christian Tradition.* New York: Simon & Schuster, 1974.

Russell, Letty M. *Church in the Round: Feminist Interpretation of the Church.* Louisville, Ky.: Westminster John Knox, 1993.

―――. *Human Liberation in a Feminist Perspective: A Theology.* Philadelphia: Westminster, 1974.

Swidler, Leonard, and Arlene Swidler, eds. *Women Priests: A Catholic Commentary on the Vatican Declaration.* New York: Paulist, 1977.

Tavard, George H. *Woman in Christian Tradition.* Notre Dame: Ind.: University of Notre Dame, 1973.

48

THE "SENSE OF THE FAITHFUL"

This section presupposes the literature presented in sections 43–47.

*Burkhard, John. "*Sensus Fidei*: Theological Reflection since Vatican II: I, 1965–1984." *Heythrop Journal* 34 (1993): 41–59. "II, 1985–1989." *Heythrop Journal* 34 (1993): 123–26.

Congar, Yves M.-J. "Quod omnes tangit, ab omnibus tractari et approbari debet." *Revue historique de droit français et étranger* 35 (1958): 210–59.

———. "The '*Sensus Fidelium*' in the Fathers." In *Lay People in the Church*, 441–43. Westminster, Md.: Newman, 1957.

———. *Tradition and Traditions*, 314–38. New York: Macmillan, 1966.

Dobbin, Edmund J. "*Sensus Fidelium* Reconsidered." *New Theology Review* 2 (1989): 48–64.

Eno, Robert B. "Consensus and Doctrine: Three Ancient Views." *Église et théologie* 9 (1978): 473–83.

Femiano, Samuel D. *Infallibility of the Laity: The Legacy of Newman*. New York: Herder and Herder, 1967.

Ford, John T. "Newman on 'Sensus Fidelium' and Mariology." *Marian Studies* 28 (1977): 120–47.

Granfield, Patrick. "Concilium and Consensus: Decision Making in Cyprian." *The Jurist* 35 (1975): 397–408.

———. "Episcopal Elections in Cyprian: Clerical and Lay Participation." *Theological Studies* 37 (1976): 41–52.

———. "The Sensus Fidelium in Episcopal Selection." In *Electing Our Own Bishops*, edited by Peter Huizing and Knut Walf, 33–38. Concilium, no. 137. Edinburgh: T & T Clark; New York: Seabury, 1980.

King, Geoffrey. "The Acceptance of Law by the Community: A Study in the Writings of Canonists and Theologians, 1500–1750." *The Jurist* 37 (1977): 233–65.

Müller, Hubert. *Der Anteil der Laien an der Bischofswahl*. Amsterdam: B. R. Grüner, 1977.

*Newman, John Henry. *On Consulting the Faithful in Matters of Doctrine*. Reprinted with an introduction by J. Coulson. New York: Sheed & Ward, 1962.

Osawa, Takeo. *Das Bischofseinsetzungsverfahren bei Cyprian: Historische Untersuchungen zu den Begriffen iudicium, suffragium, testimonium, consensus*. Bern and Frankfurt: P. Lang, 1983.

Sesboüé, Bernard. "Autorité de magistère et vie de foi ecclésiale." *Nouvelle revue théologique* 93 (1971): 337–62.

Thils, Gustave. *L'Infaillibilité du peuple chrétien in credendo: Notes de théologie posttridentine*. Paris: Desclée De Brouwer, 1963.

Thompson, William M. "*Sensus Fidelium* and Infallibility." *American Ecclesiastical Review* 167 (1973): 450–86.

*Tillard, Jean M. R. "*Sensus fidelium*." *One in Christ* 11 (1975): 2–29.

49

THE CHURCH IN THE WORLD: THE SOCIAL MISSION OF THE CHURCH

Arnold, Franz Xaver, Karl Rahner, et al. *Handbuch der Pastoraltheologie,* vol. 2/2. Freiburg: Herder, 1966. See especially the contributions of K. Rahner and J. B. Metz.

Auer, Alfons, et al. *The Christian and the World: Readings in Theology.* New York: P. J. Kenedy, 1965.

Benestad, J. Brian. *The Pursuit of a Just Social Order: Policy Statements of the U.S. Catholic Bishops.* Washington, D.C.: Ethics and Public Policy Center, 1982.

Berger, Peter L., and Richard John Neuhaus, eds. *Against the World for the World.* New York: Seabury, 1976.

Bokenkotter, Thomas. *Church and Revolution: The Quest for Social Justice in the Catholic Church.* Garden City, N.Y: Doubleday, 1998.

Bühlmann, Walbert. *With Eyes to See: Church and World in the Third Millennium.* Maryknoll, N.Y.: Orbis, 1989.

Clarke, Thomas E., ed. *Above Every Name: The Lordship of Christ and Social Systems.* New York: Paulist, 1980. Articles by M. K. Hellwig, A. Dulles, F. Cardman, J. Farrelly, and others.

Cosmao, Vincent. *Changing the Church: An Agenda for the Churches*. Maryknoll, N.Y.: Orbis, 1984.

Cushing, Richard Cardinal. *The Servant Church*. Pastoral Letter. Boston: Daughters of St. Paul, 1966.

Dorr, Donal. *Option for the Poor: A Hundred Years of Vatican Social Teaching*. Dublin: Gill & Macmillan; Maryknoll, N.Y.: Orbis, 1983.

*Fiorenza, Francis S. *Foundational Theology: Jesus and the Church*, chaps. 7 and 8. New York: Crossroad, 1984.

Gremillion, Joseph, ed. *The Gospel of Peace and Justice: Catholic Social Teaching since Pope John*. Maryknoll, N.Y.: Orbis, 1976.

Haughey, John C., ed. *The Faith that Does Justice: Examining the Christian Sources for Social Change*. New York: Paulist, 1977. Articles by A. Dulles, J. P. Langan, D. Hollenbach, and others.

Hengel, Martin. *Property and Riches in the Early Church*. Philadelphia: Fortress, 1974.

*John Paul II. *Centesimus Annus*. Encyclical. *Origins* 21 (May 16, 1991): 1, 3–24.

Marty, Martin E. *The Public Church*. New York: Crossroad, 1981.

Metz, Johannes B. *The Emergent Church*. New York: Crossroad, 1981.

———. *Faith in History and Society*. New York: Seabury, 1980.

———. *Theology of the World*. New York: Herder and Herder, 1969.

———, ed. *The Church and the World*. Concilium, no. 6. Glen Rock, N.J.: Paulist, 1965.

O'Brien, David J., and Thomas A. Shannon, eds. *Renewing the Earth: Documents on Peace, Justice, and Liberation*. Garden City, N.Y.: Doubleday Image, 1977.

Rahner, Karl. "Church and World." In *Sacramentum Mundi,* 1:346–57. New York: Herder and Herder, 1968. Reprinted in *Encyclopedia of Theology: The Concise Sacramentum Mundi,* 237–50. New York: Seabury, 1975.

Ramsey, Paul. *Who Speaks for the Church?* Nashville, Tenn.: Abingdon, 1967.

*Ratzinger, Joseph, Otto Semmelroth, et al. "Pastoral Constitution on the Church in the Modern World." *Commentary on the Documents of Vatican II,* edited by Herbert Vorgrimler, vol. 5. New York: Herder and Herder, 1969. See especially, Yves M.-J. Congar, "The Role of the Church in the Modern World" (pp. 202–23).

Ryle, Edward, ed. *The Social Mission of the Church: A Theological Reflection.* Washington, D.C.: Catholic University of America, 1972.

Santa Ana, Julio de. *Towards a Church of the Poor: The Work of an Ecumenical Group on the Church and the Poor.* Maryknoll, N.Y.: Orbis, 1981.

Schillebeeckx, Edward. *God the Future of Man.* New York: Sheed & Ward, 1968.

————. *The Mission of the Church.* New York: Seabury, 1973.

————. *World and Church.* New York: Sheed & Ward, 1971.

Yoder, John Howard. *The Politics of Jesus.* Grand Rapids, Mich.: Wm. B. Eerdmans, 1972.

50

LIBERATION ECCLESIOLOGY

This section does not give a complete listing of the theology of liberation. We have selected those works that have a specific ecclesiological content.

Assmann, Hugo. *Theology for a Nomad Church*. Maryknoll, N.Y.: Orbis, 1976.

Between Honesty and Hope: Documents From and About the Church in Latin America. Maryknoll, N.Y.: Orbis, 1976.

Boff, Leonardo. *Church: Charism and Power*. New York: Crossroad, 1985.

Boff, Leonardo, and Clodovis Boff. *Introducing Liberation Theology*. Maryknoll, N.Y.: Orbis, 1987.

Brown, Robert McAfee. *Liberation Theology: An Introductory Guide*. Louisville, Ky.: Westminster John Knox, 1993.

*———. *Theology in a New Key: Responding to Liberation Themes*. Philadelphia: Westminster, 1978.

Cadorette, Curt, et al. *Liberation Theology: An Introductory Reader*. Maryknoll, N.Y.: Orbis, 1992.

*Congregation for the Doctrine of the Faith. "Instruction on Certain Aspects of the Theology of Liberation." *Origins* 24 (Sept. 13, 1984): 193–204.

————. "Instruction on Christian Freedom and Liberation." *Origins* 15 (April 17, 1986): 713, 715–28.

Dussel, Enrique. *History and the Theology of Liberation.* Maryknoll, N.Y.: Orbis, 1976.

————. *A History of the Church in Latin America: Colonialism to Liberation (1492–1979).* Grand Rapids, Mich.: Wm. B. Eerdmans, 1982.

Eagleson, John, and Philip Scharper. *Puebla and Beyond.* Maryknoll, N.Y.: Orbis, 1979.

Elizondo, Virgil, and Norbert Greinacher, eds. *Tensions between the Churches of the First World and the Third World.* Concilium, no. 144. New York: Seabury, 1981.

*Ellacuría, Ignacio, and Jon Sobrino, eds. *Mysterium Liberationis: Fundamental Concepts of Liberation Theology.* Maryknoll, N.Y.: Orbis, 1993.

Ferm, Deane William. *Profiles in Liberation: 36 Portraits of Third World Theologians.* Mystic, Conn.: Twenty-Third, 1988.

Gibellini, Rosino, ed. *Frontiers of Theology in Latin America.* Maryknoll, N.Y.: Orbis, 1979.

*Gutiérrez, Gustavo. *A Theology of Liberation: History, Politics, and Salvation.* Rev. ed. New introduction. Maryknoll, N.Y.: Orbis, 1988.

Gutiérrez, Gustavo, and R. Schaull. *Liberation and Change.* Atlanta: John Knox, 1977.

Haight, Roger. *An Alternative Vision: An Interpretation of Liberation Theology.* New York: Paulist, 1985.

Hennelly, Alfred T. *Liberation Theologies: The Global Pursuit of Justice.* Mystic, Conn.: Twenty- Third, 1995.

*————. *Liberation Theology: A Documentary History.* Maryknoll, N.Y.: Orbis, 1990.

————. *Theologies in Conflict: The Challenge of Juan Luis Segundo*. Maryknoll, N.Y.: Orbis, 1979.

————. *Theology for a Liberating Church: The New Praxis of Freedom*. Washington, D.C.: Georgetown University, 1989.

————, ed. *Santo Domingo and Beyond: Documents and Commentaries from the Historic Meeting of the Latin American Bishops' Conference*. Maryknoll, N.Y.: Orbis, 1993.

International Theological Commission. "Human Development and Christian Salvation." *Origins* 7 (Nov. 3, 1977): 305–13. Also in *International Theological Commission, Texts and Documents 1969–1985*. San Francisco: Ignatius, 1989, 145–61.

Kloppenburg, Bonaventure. *The People's Church*. Chicago: Franciscan Herald, 1978.

Latin American Episcopal Council (CELAM). *The Church in the Present-Day Transformation of Latin America in the Light of the Council: Conclusions*. The Medellín Conference. Bogota: General Secretariat of CELAM, 1970.

————. *III General Conference of Latin American Bishops, Evangelization at Present and in the Future of Latin America*. The Puebla Conference. Washington, D.C.: NCCB, 1979.

Laurentin, René. *Liberation, Development, and Salvation*. Maryknoll, N.Y.: Orbis, 1972.

Magaña, Alvaro Quiroz. *Eclesiologia en la teologia de la liberación*. Salamanca: Sígueme, 1983.

Mahan, Brian, and L. Dale Richesin, eds. *The Challenge of Liberation Theology: A First World Response*. Maryknoll, N.Y.: Orbis, 1981.

McCann, Dennis. *Christian Realism and Liberation Theology: Practical Theologies in Creative Conflict*. Maryknoll, N.Y.: Orbis, 1981.

McGovern, Arthur F. *Liberation Theology and Its Critics: Toward an Assessment.* Maryknoll, N.Y.: Orbis, 1989.

————. *Marxism: An American Christian Perspective.* Maryknoll, N.Y.: Orbis, 1980.

Miguez Bonino, José. *Doing Theology in a Revolutionary Situation.* Philadelphia: Fortress, 1975.

*Musto, Ronald G. *Liberation Theologies: A Research Guide.* New York and London: Garland, 1991.

Nealen, Mary Kaye. *The Poor in the Ecclesiology of Juan Luis Segundo.* New York: Peter Lang, 1991.

Novak, Michael. *Will It Liberate? Questions about Liberation Theology.* New York: Paulist, 1986.

O'Brien, John. *Theology and the Option for the Poor.* Collegeville, Minn.: Liturgical Press, 1992.

Ogden, Schubert M. *Faith and Freedom: Towards a Theology of Liberation.* Nashville, Tenn.: Abingdon, 1979.

Quade, Quentin L., ed. *The Pope and Revolution: John Paul II Confronts Liberation Theology.* Washington, D.C.: Ethics and Public Policy Center, 1982.

Ruether, Rosemary Radford. *Liberation Theology.* New York: Paulist, 1972.

Schall, James V. *Liberation Theology in Latin America.* San Francisco: Ignatius, 1982.

Segundo, Juan Luis. *Faith and Ideologies.* Maryknoll, N.Y.: Orbis, 1984.

————. *The Hidden Motives of Pastoral Action.* Maryknoll, N.Y.: Orbis, 1978.

————. *The Liberation of Theology.* Maryknoll, N.Y.: Orbis, 1976.

————. *Theology and the Church: A Response to Cardinal Ratzinger and a Warning to the Whole Church*. Minneapolis: Winston, 1985.

*————. *A Theology for Artisans of a New Humanity*. Vol. 1, *The Community Called Church*. Maryknoll, N.Y.: Orbis; Dublin: Gill & Macmillan, 1973.

Smith, Christian. *The Emergence of Liberation Theology: Radical Religion and Social Movement Theory*. Chicago: University of Chicago, 1991.

Sobrino, Jon. *The True Church and the Poor*. Maryknoll, N.Y.: Orbis, 1984.

Torres, Sergio, and John Eagleson, eds. *Theology in the Americas*. Maryknoll, N.Y.: Orbis, 1976.

51

THE MULTICULTURAL CHURCH

A. General Studies

Bevans, Stephen. *Models of Contextual Theology*. Maryknoll, N.Y.: Orbis, 1992.

Chupungco, Anscar. *Liturgies of the Future: The Process and Methods of Inculturation*. New York: Paulist, 1989.

Congregation for Divine Worship and the Discipline of the Sacraments. "The Roman Liturgy and Inculturation." *Origins* 25 (April 14, 1994): 745, 747–56.

Fitzpatrick, Joseph P. *One Church Many Cultures: The Challenge of Diversity*. Kansas City, Mo.: Sheed & Ward, 1987.

International Theological Commission. "Faith and Inculturation." *Origins* 18 (May 4, 1989): 800–807.

*Phan, Peter C. "Contemporary Theology and Inculturation in the United States." In *The Multicultural Church: A New Landscape in U.S. Theologies,* edited by William Cenkner, 109–30. New York and Mahwah, N.J.: Paulist, 1996.

Schineller, Peter. *A Handbook on Inculturation*. New York and Mahwah, N.J.: Paulist, 1990.

Schreiter, Robert J. *Constructing Local Theologies*. Maryknoll, N.Y.: Orbis, 1985.

———. *The New Catholicity: Theology between the Global and the Local*. Maryknoll, N.Y.: Orbis, 1997.

Shorter, Aylward. *Toward a Theology of Inculturation*. Maryknoll, N.Y.: Orbis, 1988.

B. Hispanic/Latino Ecclesiology

Bañuelas, Arturo J., ed. *Mestizo Christianity: Theology from the Latino Perspective*. Maryknoll, N.Y.: Orbis, 1995.

Casarella, Peter, and Raul Gomez, eds. *El Cuerpo de Cristo. The Hispanic Presence in the U. S. Catholic Church*. New York: Crossroad, 1998.

Cook, Guillermo, ed. *New Face of the Church in Latin America*. Maryknoll, N.Y.: Orbis, 1994.

Deck, Allan Figueroa, Yolanda Tarago, and Timothy M. Matovina. *Perspectivas: Hispanic Ministry*. Kansas City, Mo.: Sheed & Ward, 1995.

*Deck, Allan Figueroa, ed. *Frontiers of Hispanic Theology in the United States*. Maryknoll, N.Y.: Orbis, 1992.

Elizondo, Virgilio. *Christianity and Culture: An Introduction to Pastoral Theology and Ministry in the Bicultural Community*. San Antonio: Mexican American Cultural Center, 1975.

Espín, Orlando. "A Multicultural Church: Theological Reflections from Below." In *The Multicultural Church: A New Landscape in U.S. Theologies,* edited by William Cenkner, 54–71. New York and Mahwah, N.J.: Paulist, 1996.

García, Ismael. "Theological and Ethical Reflections on the Church as a Community of Resistance." *Journal of Hispanic/Latino Theology* 4 (1996): 6–33.

*Goizueta, Roberto S. *Caminemos con Jésus: Toward a Hispanic/Latino Theology of Accompaniment.* Maryknoll, N.Y.: Orbis, 1995.

González, Justo L. *Mañana: Christian Theology from a Hispanic Perspective.* Nashville, Tenn.: Abingdon, 1990.

*González, Roberto O., and Michael LaVelle. *The Hispanic Catholic in the United States: A Socio-Cultural and Religious Profile.* New York: Northeast Catholic Pastoral Center for Hispanics, 1985.

Isasi-Díaz, Ada María. *Mujerista Theology: A Theology for the Twenty-First Century.* Maryknoll, N.Y.: Orbis, 1996.

Linan, John E. "Basic Church Communities in the Mexican American and Mexican Community and their Ecclesiological Significance." In *Dialogue Rejoined: Theology and Ministry in the United States Hispanic Reality,* edited by Ana Maria Pineda and Robert Schreiter, 99–124. Collegeville, Minn.: Liturgical Press, 1995.

Martínez, Dolorita. "Basic Christian Communities: A New Model of Church within the U.S. Hispanic Community." *New Theology Review* 3 (1990): 35–42.

Nickoloff, James B. "A 'Church of the Poor' in the Sixteenth Century: The Ecclesiology of Bartolome de las Casas' De unico modo," *Journal of Hispanic/Latino Theology* 2 (1995): 26–40.

Rosado, Caleb. "The Church, the City, and the Compassionate Christ." In *Voces: Voices from the Hispanic Church,* edited by Justo L. González, 71–80. Nashville, Tenn.: Abingdon, 1992.

C. African and African-American Ecclesiology

Cone, James H. *Black Theology and Black Power.* New York: Seabury, 1969.

*————. *A Black Theology of Liberation: Twentieth Anniversary Edition.* Maryknoll, N.Y.: Orbis, 1990.

————. *For My People: Black Theology and the Black Church.* Maryknoll, N.Y.: Orbis, 1984.

————. *God of the Oppressed.* New York: Seabury, 1975.

————. *Speaking the Truth: Ecumenism, Liberation, and Black Theology.* Grand Rapids, Mich.: Wm. B. Eerdmans, 1986.

Cone, James H., and Gayraud S. Wilmore, eds. *Black Theology: A Documentary History.* 2 vols. Vol. 1, 1966–1979; Vol. 2, 1980–1992. Maryknoll, N.Y.: Orbis, 1993.

Gardiner, James J., and J. Deotis Roberts, eds. *Quest for a Black Theology.* Philadelphia: Fortress, 1974.

Gibellini, Rosino, ed. *Paths of African Theology.* Maryknoll, N.Y.: Orbis, 1994.

*Hayes, Diana L. *And Still We Rise: An Introduction to Black Liberation Theology.* New York and Mahwah, N.J.: Paulist, 1996.

Hillman, Eugene. *Toward an African Christianity: Inculturation Applied.* New York and Mahwah, N.J.: Paulist, 1993.

Oduyoye, Mercy Amba. *Hearing and Knowing: Theological Reflections on Christianity in Africa.* Maryknoll, N.Y.: 1986.

Oduyoye, Mercy Amba, and Musimbi A. Kanyora, eds. *The Will to Arise: Women, Tradition, and the Church in Africa.* Maryknoll, N.Y.: Orbis, 1992.

Uzukwu, Elochukwu E. *A Listening Church: Autonomy and Communion in African Churches.* Maryknoll, N.Y.: Orbis, 1996.

D. Asian Ecclesiology

*Amaladoss, Michael. *Making All Things New: Dialogue, Pluralism, and Evangelization in Asia.* Maryknoll, N.Y.: Orbis, 1990.

Chang, Aloysius B. "The Church in China: Ecclesiological Impasse? A Christological and Trinitarian Approach Towards a Solution." *Tripod* 12 (1992): 60-69.

―――. "Fundamental Attitude of the Bridge Church." *The Japan Missionary Bulletin* 45 (1991): 239–49.

Chung, Hyun Kyung. *Struggle to Be the Sun Again: Introducing Asian Women's Theology.* Maryknoll, N.Y.: Orbis, 1990.

Dupuis, Jacques. "Evangelization and Kingdom Values: The Church and the 'Others'." *Indian Missiological Review* 14 (1992): 4–22.

Lee, Jung Young. "Authentic Church: The Community of New Marginality." In J. Y. Lee, *Marginality: The Key to Multicultural Theology*, 121–47. Minneapolis: Fortress, 1995.

Lim, Byeung-Hun. "A Study on Ecclesiological Foundations of Evangelization in the 21st Century." *Catholic Theology and Thought* 7 (1992): 71–89.

Mercado, Edwin E. "Emerging Images of the Asian Church." *Philippina Sacra* 26 (1991): 77–94.

Pathil, Kuncheria. "The Vision of an Ecumenical Church." *Jeevadhara* 21 (1991): 316-23.

Pieris, Aloysius. "Mission of the Local Church in Relation to Other Major Religious Traditions." *The Month* 15 (1982): 81–90.

Rosales, Gaudencio B., and C. G. Arévalo, eds. *For All the Peoples of Asia: Federation of Asian Bishops' Conferences. Documents from 1970 to 1991.* Maryknoll, N.Y.: Orbis, 1992.

Song, Choan-Seng. *Jesus and the Reign of God.* Minneapolis: Fortress, 1993.

Sugirtharajah, R. S., ed. *Frontiers in Asian Christian Theology.*

E. Native American Ecclesiology

Hultkrantz, Ake. *Native Religions of North America*. New York: Harper & Row, 1997.

Las Casas, Bartolomé de. *The Only Way*. Edited by Helen Parish and translated by Francis Sullivan. New York and Mahwah, N.J.: Paulist, 1992.

*Starkloff, Carl F. "'Evangelization' and Native Americans." *Studies in the International Apostolate of the Jesuits*, 4/1:1–37. Washington, D.C.: Jesuit Missions, 1975.

———. "Mission Method and the American Indian." *Theological Studies* 38 (1977): 621–53.

———. "Native Americans and the Catholic Church." In *The Encyclopedia of American Catholic History*, 1009–1020. Collegeville, Minn.: Liturgical, 1997.

———. *The People of the Center: American Indian Religion and Christianity*. New York: Seabury, 1974.

Sullivan, Lawrence E., ed. *Native American Religions: North America*. New York: Macmillan, 1989.

Thwaites, Reuben Gold, ed. *Jesuit Relations and Allied Documents*. 73 vols. Cleveland: Burrows Brothers, 1896–1901. Reprint, New York: Pageant, 1959.

Vecsey, Christopher. *American Indian Catholics: On the Padres' Trail*. Notre Dame, Ind.: University of Notre Dame, 1996.

———. *The Paths of Kateri's Kin*. Notre Dame, Ind.: University of Notre Dame, 1998.

52

MARY AND THE CHURCH

Rivera, A. "Bibliografía sobre Maria, Madre de la Iglesia." *Ephemerides Mariologicae* 32 (1981): 265–71.

· · ·

Anderson, H. George, J. Francis Stafford, and Joseph A. Burgess, eds. *The One Mediator, the Saints, and Mary*. Lutherans and Catholics in Dialogue, vol. 8. Minneapolis: Augsburg, 1992.

*Balthasar, Hans Urs von. *Theo-Drama,* 3:292–360. San Francisco: Ignatius, 1992.

Beinert, Wolfgang, and Heinrich Petri, eds. *Handbuch der Marienkunde*. Regensburg: Pustet, 1984.

Cantalamessa, Reniero. *Mary, Mirror of the Church*. Collegeville, Minn.: Liturgical Press, 1992.

Congar, Yves M.-J. "Marie et l'Église dans la pensée patristique." *Revue des sciences philosophiques et théologiques* 38 (1954): 3–38.

Dander, Franz. *Kleine Marienkunde*. Innsbruck: Tyrolia, 1960.

Galot, Jean. "Marie, type et modéle de l'Église." In *L'Église de Vatican II,* edited by Guilherme Baraúna, 3:1243–59. Unam Sanctam 51c. Paris: Cerf, 1966. Italian version: *La Chiesa del Vaticano II*. Florence: Vallecchi, 1965. German version: *De*

Ecclesia: Beiträge zur Konstitution über die Kirche des II. Vatikanischen Konzils. Freiburg: Herder, 1966.

———. "Théologie du titre 'mère de l'Église.'" *Ephemerides Mariologicae* 32 (1982): 159–73.

John Paul II. Encyclical Letter *Origins* 16 (April 9, 1987): 745, 747–66. *The Mother of the Redeemer: Redemptoris Mater.*

Laurentin, René. *Mary's Place in the Church.* London: Burns & Oates, 1965.

*Lubac, Henri de. *The Splendour of the Church,* 238–89. New York: Sheed & Ward, 1956. Reprint, *The Splendor of the Church,* 315–80. San Francisco: Ignatius, 1991.

Maria et Ecclesia: Acta Congressus Mariologici-Mariani in Civitate Lourdes Anno 1958 Celebrati. 16 vols. Rome: Academia Mariana Internationalis, 1959–62.

Meo, Salvatore M., ed. *Maria e la chiesa oggi: Atti del 5 simposio mariologico internazionale (Rome, 1984).* Bologna: Marianum & Dehoniane, 1985.

Müller, Alois. *Ecclesia-Maria: Die Einheit Marias und der Kirche.* 2nd ed. Freiburg: Universitätsverlag, 1955.

Piolanti, Antonio. *Maria e il Corpo Mistico.* Rome: Angelo Belardetti, 1957.

Rahner, Hugo. *Our Lady and the Church.* New York: Pantheon, 1961.

Ratzinger, Joseph. *Daughter Zion: Meditations on the Church's Marian Belief.* San Francisco: Ignatius, 1983.

Schillebeeckx, Edward, and Catharina Malkes. *Mary: Yesterday, Today, Tomorrow.* New York: Crossroad, 1983.

*Semmelroth, Otto. *Mary, Archtype of the Church.* New York: Sheed & Ward, 1963.

Stacpoole, Alberic, ed. *Mary and the Churches.* Collegeville, Minn.: Liturgical Press, 1987. Articles by Mary Anne DeTrana, Eamon R. Carroll, Kevin McDonald, and others.

Tavard, George H. *The Thousand Faces of the Virgin Mary.* Collegeville, Minn.: Liturgical Press, 1996.

Vollert, Cyril. "Mary and the Church." In *Mariology,* edited by Juniper B. Carol, 2:550–95. Milwaukee, Wis.: Bruce, 1957.

53

THE CHURCH, THE KINGDOM, AND THE ESCHATON

Bright, John. *Kingdom of God: The Biblical Concept and Its Meaning for the Church*. Nashville, Tenn.: Abingdon, 1953.

Corell, Alf. *Consummatum est: Eschatology and Church in the Gospel of John*. London: SPCK, 1958.

Cullmann, Oscar. "The Kingship of Christ and the Church in the New Testament." In *The Early Church*, 105–37. Philadelphia: Westminster, 1956.

*Dulles, Avery. "The Church as Eschatological Community." In *The Eschaton: A Community of Love*, edited by J. Papin, 4:69–103. Villanova University Symposium. Philadelphia: Villanova University, 1971.

Fuellenbach, John. *The Kingdom of God: The Message of Jesus Today*. Maryknoll, N.Y.: Orbis, 1995.

Gennadios, Limouris, ed. *Church, Kingdom, Word: The Church as Mystery and Prophetic Sign*. Faith and Order Paper no. 130. Geneva: World Council of Churches, 1986.

Haughey, John C. "Church and Kingdom: Ecclesiology in the Light of Eschatology." *Theological Studies* 29 (1968): 72–86.

McBrien, Richard P. *Do We Need the Church?* New York: Harper & Row, 1969.

Niebuhr, H. Richard. *The Kingdom of God in America.* New York: Harper Torchbooks, 1959.

*Pannenberg, Wolfhart. *Theology and the Kingdom of God.* Philadelphia: Westminster, 1969.

Perrin, Norman. *Jesus and the Language of the Kingdom.* Philadelphia: Fortress, 1976.

————. *The Kingdom of God in the Preaching of Jesus.* Philadelphia: Westminster, 1963.

Ruether, Rosemary Radford. *The Radical Kingdom: The Western Experience of Messianic Hope.* New York: Harper & Row, 1970.

Schmidt, Karl Ludwig. *Basileia: Bible Key Words from Kittel.* London: A. & C. Black, 1957.

Schnackenburg, Rudolf. "Church and Parousia." In *One, Holy, Catholic and Apostolic Church,* edited by Herbert Vorgrimler, 91–134. New York: Herder and Herder, 1968.

*————. *God's Rule and Kingdom.* New York: Herder and Herder, 1965.

Schönborn, Christoph. "The Kingdom of God and the Heavenly-Earthly Church: The Church in Transition according to *Lumen Gentium.*" In *From Death to Life: The Christian Journey,* 65–98. San Francisco: Ignatius, 1995.

Skydsgaard, Kristen E. "The Kingdom of God and the Church." *Scottish Journal of Theology* 4 (1951): 383–97.

Stanley, David M. "Kingdom to Church." In *The Apostolic Church in the New Testament,* 5–37. Westminster, Md.: Newman, 1965.

Viviano, Benedict T. *The Kingdom of God in History.* Wilmington, Del.: Michael Glazier, 1988.

INDEX OF NAMES

Acerbi, Antonio, 41, 91
Ackley, John B., 55
Adam, Karl, 17
Adolfs, Robert, 46
Afanassieff, Nicolas, 51
Afonso, Meneo A., 102
Agrimson, J. Elmo, 140
Ahern, B., 44, 65
Alberigo, Giuseppe, 29, 36, 41, 42, 43, 107, 126, 133
Alesandro, J. A., 121
Alfaro, Juan, 118
Allen, Joseph J., 51
Allmen, Jean Jacques von, 107, 132
Alston, Wallace M., Jr., 55
Amaladoss, Michael, 173
Amato, Angelo, 132
Anciaux, Paul, 113
Anderson, Gerald H., 83
Anderson, H. George, 10, 176
Antón, Angel, 36, 42, 46, 59, 129
Appleby, R. Scott, 112, 137

Aquino, María Pillar, 157
Arbuckle, Gerald A., 149
Arévalo, C. G., 174
Arnau-García, Ramon, 29
Arnold, Franz Xaver, 86, 136, 154, 162
Arquillière, H.-X., 17
Ashe, Kaye, 157
Ashley, Benedict M., 157
Asmussen, Hans, 64
Assmann, Hugo, 165
Astorri, Romeo, 129
At, Jean-Antoine, 36
Aubert, Roger, 30, 37, 38, 47
Auer, Alfons, 162
Auer, Johann, 10, 59
Aulén, Gustav, 55, 57
Avis, Paul D., 34, 55, 91
Azevedo, Marcello deC., 94, 149

Bacik, James J., 46
Backman, Milton V., Jr., 72
Baier, Walter, 10

Balch, David L., 23

Balthasar, Hans Urs von, 27, 69, 79, 107, 143, 149, 176

Banks, Robert J., 20

Bantle, Franz Xaver, 123

Bañuelas, Arturo J., 171

Baraúna, Guilherme, 42, 67, 90, 134, 141, 176

Barbé, Dominique, 94

Bárczay, Gyula, 36

Bardy, Gustave, 25

Baril, Gilberte, 59

Barreau, Jean Claude, 137

Barreiro, Alvaro, 94

Barrois, Georges Augustin, 51

Barta, Russell, 152

Barth, Karl, 42, 55

Bartlett, David L., 143

Bassett, William, 105, 150

Batiffol, Pierre, 107

Baum, Gregory, 43, 46, 73, 77, 97, 102

Bäumer, Remigius, 10, 66, 109

Bausch, William J., 136

Bavel, T. J. van, 27

Bazatole, B., 132

Bea, Augustin, 73, 74

Beal, J., 100

Beales, Derek, 10

Becker, Werner, 74

Beinert, Wolfgang, 66, 132, 176

Bellarminus, Robertus, 17

Benestad, J. Brian, 162

Benko, Stephen, 91

Benoit, Pierre, 20

Benz, Ernst, 51

Berger, Peter L., 102, 162

Berkouwer, Gerrit C., 42, 56

Bermejo, Luis M., 74, 123

Bernardin, Joseph, 100

Bernier, Paul, 143

Bertrams, Wilhelm, 113

Best, Geoffrey, 10

Best, Thomas F., 93

Betti, Umberto, 36, 38, 113

Bevans, Stephen B., 87, 170

Beyer, Jean, 149, 154

Bianchi, Eugene C., 100

Biffi, Giacomo, 69

Billot, Ludovicus, 17

Birbeck, W. J., 53

Birkey, Del, 20

Bissonnette, Tomás G., 92, 94

Black, Antony, 29

Blane, A., 52

Blauw, Johannes, 83

Blöchlinger, Alex, 136

Blockx, Karel, 5

Blumenthal, Uta-Renate, 29

Bockmuehl, Markus, 10

Boff, Clodovis, 94, 165

Boff, Leonardo, 88, 94, 152, 165

Bohr, David, 83, 86

Bokenkotter, Thomas, 162

Bonhoeffer, Dietrich, 56

Bonner, Gerald, 27

Bordelon, Marvin, 136

Borders, W. D., 115

Borelli, John, 51

Borgomeo, Pasquale, 27

Bosc, J., 66

Bosch, David J., 83

Botte, Bernard, 126

Bouëssé, Humbert, 113

Boulard, F., 117
Bourgeois, H., 50
Bourke, Myles M., 20
Bouyer, Louis, 19, 59, 157
Bowe, Barbara, 25
Boyack, Kenneth, 137
Boyle, John P., 118, 121
Braaten, Carl E., 74, 83
Brandenburg, Albert, 107
Branick, Vincent P., 20
Bravi, Maurizio Claudio, 129
Braxton, Edward K., 46
Brechter, Suso, 84
Brennan, Patrick J., 136
Bria, Ion, 51, 72
Brière, Yves de la, 66
Bright, John, 179
Broderick, John F., 38
Broucker, José de, 46
Brown, Raymond E., 20, 107, 118, 134, 143
Brown, Robert McAfee, 74, 165
Brunner, Emil, 56
Buckley, Mary I., 102
Buckley, Michael J., 108
Bühlmann, Walbert, 59, 84, 162
Bulgakov, Sergei Nikolayev, 51
Burgess, Joseph A., 71, 74, 110, 119, 176
Burgess, Stanley M., 140
Burghardt, Walter J., 65, 81
Burke, Mary, 126
Burkhard, John, 160
Burn-Murdoch, Hector, 108
Burns, J. P., 81
Burns, Patrick J., 9, 102, 126

Burrows, William R., 84, 143
Burtchaell, James T., 21
Butler, Basil Christopher, 42, 59, 74, 123
Butler, Cuthbert, 38
Butler, Sara, 157
Byrne, Patricia, 137

Cada, Lawrence, 149
Cadorette, Curt, 165
Camelot, P. T., 19, 126
Campbell, Debra, 137
Campenhausen, Hans von., 21, 25
Camps, A., 87
Cantalamessa, Reniero, 176
Capocci, Giacomo, 17
Caprile, Giovanni, 129
Cardman, F., 43, 162
Carlen, Claudia, 14, 15
Carlson, R. J., 121
Carmody, Denise Lardner, 10, 60
Carmody, John Tully, 10, 60
Carol, Juniper B., 178
Carr, Anne E., 157
Carrier, Hervé, 79
Carroll, Eamon R., 178
Casarella, Peter, 171
Casel, Odo, 60
Castelli, Enrico, 123
Castelli, Jim, 138
Cenkner, William, 170, 171
Cerfaux, Lucien, 21
Chaillet, Pierre, 36
Chamberlain, Gary, 114
Chang, Aloysius B., 173, 174
Chavasse, A., 124

Cheng, Tsan-Yuang, 147
Chenu, M.-D., 43
Chica, F., 10
Chirico, Peter, 100, 123
Chittister, Joan, 157
Chodorow, Stanley, 29
Chung, Hyun Kyung, 174
Chupungco, Anscar, 170
Citrini, T., 50
Clark, Elizabeth A., 158
Clark, Stephen B., 95
Clarke, Thomas E., 149, 162
Clarkson, J. E., 15
Clément, Olivier, 52
Cody, Aelred, 21
Coleman, John A., 86, 102, 152
Collins, Mary, 152
Colombo, C., 44
Colombo, G., 47
Colonna, Egidio. *See* Giles of Rome
Colson, Jean, 25, 113
Comblin, Joseph, 84
Concetti, Gino, 114, 130
Cone, James H., 172, 173
Congar, Yves M.-J., 5, 19, 29, 30, 32, 34, 37, 42, 43, 44, 46, 60, 64, 66, 67, 69, 74, 79, 81, 88, 97, 100, 108, 113, 117, 118, 122, 126, 129, 132, 140, 143, 148, 151, 152, 153, 160, 164, 176
Connan, Francis, 137
Constantelos, Demetrios J., 52
Contri, Antonio, 132
Conway, Eamonn, 81

Conzemius, V., 61
Cook, Guillermo, 95, 171
Cooke, Bernard, 65, 108, 143
Cope, Brian E., 76
Cordes, Paul J., 144
Corecco, Eugenio, 105
Corell, Alf, 179
Coriden, James A., 105, 115, 130, 131, 137
Cosmao, Vincent, 163
Costas, Orlando E., 84
Coste, René, 42
Costello, Gerald M., 95
Costigan, Richard F., 36, 123
Cote, Richard G., 84
Cotter, James P., 84
Cottier, Georges, 69
Coulson, J., 161
Cowan, Michael A., 95, 144
Cox, H., 110
Crumley, James R., 10
Cullmann, Oscar, 21, 42, 74, 75, 108, 179
Culpepper, Robert H., 140
Cunningham, Agnes, 114
Curran, Charles E., 105, 118, 119, 120, 133
Cusack, Barbara Anne, 137
Cushing, Richard Cardinal, 163
Cussiánovich, Alejandro, 150
Cwiekowski, Frederick J., 21

Dabin, Paul, 153
Dallen, James, 144
Daly, Robert J., 150
Damaskinos, M., 52
Dander, Franz, 176

Daniélou, Jean, 11, 25, 28, 60
D'Antonio, William V., 153
Davidson, James D., 153
Davies, John G., 21, 84
Davis, Charles, 137
Davis, R., 110
Dearden, J., 115
Deck, Allan Figueroa, 171
Defois, Gérard, 97, 98
De Graeve, F., 127
Dejaifve, Georges, 38, 39, 43, 79, 124
Delahaye, Karl, 25
Delaruelle, Étienne, 30
Delespesse, Max, 95
Delhaye, Philippe, 41
Delorme, Jean, 144
Denzler, Georg, 108
Descamps, A. L., 119
DeSiano, Frank, 137
Desjardins, R., 27
DeTrana, Mary Anne, 178
Dhavamony, Mariasusai, 84
Dianich, Severino, 50, 60
Dias, P. V., 19
Dick, John A., 75
Dietrich, Donald J., 37
DiNoia, J. A., 86
Dinter, Paul E., 144
Dionne, J. Robert, 108
Dirkswager, Edward J., 9
Dix, Gregory, 108
Dobbin, Edmund J., 160
Doignon, J., 69
Dolan, Jay P., 43, 100, 137
Dolch, Heimo, 10, 66
Dombois, Hans, 97
Donfried, Karl P., 21, 107

Donovan, Daniel, 47, 60, 144
Donovan, Vincent J., 84
Doohan, Leonard, 152, 153
Doré, J., 121
Dóriga, Enrique L., 60, 114
Dorr, Donal, 163
Dortel-Claudot, Michel, 133
Downs, Thomas, 137
Doyle, Dennis M., 43
Drane, James F., 105
Drilling, Peter, 144
Droel, William L., 153
Duffy, S., 43
Dulles, Avery, 32, 43, 47, 60, 67, 75, 79, 86, 88, 91, 97, 100, 110, 118, 119, 131, 144, 162, 163, 179
Dumas, A., 122
Dunn, James D. G., 21
Dupuis, Jacques, 154, 174
Dupuy, Bernard-Dominique, 5, 114, 132
Duquoc, Christian, 75, 122, 140
Dussel, Enrique, 166
Dvornik, Francis, 127, 129
Dyer, George J., 133
Dyer, Ralph J., 150
Dyson, R. W., 17

Eagan, Joseph F., 47
Eagleson, John, 96, 166, 169
Ebeling, Gerhard, 56
Edelby, Neophytos, 141
Efroymson, David, 11
Eicher, P., 120
Eldern, Marlin van, 72
Elert, Werner, 88

Elizondo, Virgilio, 94, 158, 166, 171
Ellacuría, Ignacio, 166
Ellis, J. T., 154
Ellis, Mark H., 11
Eminyan, Maurice, 81
Empie, Paul C., 76, 108, 119, 126
Eno, Robert B., 27, 108, 119, 127, 160
Erb, Peter C., 18
Erickson, John H., 51, 52
Ermath, Margaret Sittler, 158
Ernst, Cornelius, 108
Ernst, Josef, 133
Espín, Orlando, 171
Estevez, Medina, 44
Evans, Gillian R., 11, 75
Evans, Robert F., 25
Evdokimov, Paul, 52

Fagin, Gerald M., 43
Fagiolo, Vincenzo, 114, 130
Fahey, Michael A., 47, 49, 52, 72, 75, 92, 134
Faivre, Alexandre, 153
Farmer, Jerry T., 144
Farmer, William R., 108
Farrelly, J., 162
Faul, D., 27
Feiner, Johannes, 23, 67, 74
Feliciani, Giorgio, 130
Femiano, Samuel D., 160
Fenhagen, James, 153
Fenton, Joseph C., 81
Ferguson, Everett, 21
Ferm, Deane William, 166
Fesquet, Henri, 45, 130

Fessler, J., 39
Fèvre, Justinus, 17
Fey, Harold E., 72
Fichter, Joseph, 103, 140
Finson, Shelley Davis, 157
Fiorenza, Elisabeth Schüssler, 158
Fiorenza, Francis Schüssler, 21, 47, 163
Fitzpatrick, Joseph P., 170
Fjeld, Roger W., 117
Flanagan, Padraig, 84
Flannery, Austin, 16
Flew, Robert Newton, 75
Flood, Edmund, 153
Floristan, Casiano, 137, 140
Florovsky, Georges, 52
Fogarty, Gerald P., 108, 114
Foley, Gerald, 137, 154
Fontaine, Gaston, 17
Ford, David F., 5
Ford, John C., 119
Ford, John T., 75, 124, 161
Forell, George W., 35
Forster, Patricia, 139
Forte, Bruno, 60, 88
Fouilloux, Etienne, 47
Fox, Zeni, 154
Fraling, Bernhard, 11
Franco, E., 92
Fransen, Piet, 41, 43, 122, 127
Franzelin, Johannes B., 17
Franzen, August, 30, 109
Fraser, Ian, 95
Fraser, Margaret, 95
Fridrichsen, Anton, 55, 57
Fries, Heinrich, 43, 61, 75, 100
Frisque, Jean, 47

Fuellenbach, John, 109, 179
Fürer, I., 131

Gager, John G., 21
Gagnebet, Rosarius, 114
Gaillardetz, Richard R., 119, 124
Galot, Jean, 64, 144, 158, 176, 177
Galvin, John P., 47, 49, 92, 109
Ganoczy, Alexandre, 34
García, Ismael, 171
Garciadiego, Alejandro, 67
Gardiner, James J., 173
Garijo-Guembe, Miguel M., 61, 92
Garuti, Adriano S., 109
Gasser, Vinzenz, 124
Gassmann, Benno, 34
Gassmann, Günther, 11, 93
Gaudem, J., 98
Gaudemet, J., 114
Geaney, Dennis J., 137
Geerlings, Wilhelm, 11
Geffré, Claude, 11
Geiselmann, J. R., 18
Gelpi, Donald L., 140, 150
Gennadios, Limouris, 179
George, F. E., 86
Gerth, H. H., 104
Ghirlanda, Gianfranco, 114
Gibellini, Rosino, 166, 173
Giblet, Jean, 21
Giles of Rome, 17
Gilkey, Langdon, 56
Gill, Robin, 103
Giordano, Pasquale B., 85
Giussani, Luigi, 47

Glasser, Arthur F., 85
Goizueta, Roberto S., 172
Goldie, Rosemary, 152
Gomez, Raul, 171
González, Justo L. 172
González, Roberto O., 172
González Faus, José I., 105
Goulder, M. D., 124
Gourgues, Michel, 11
Grabmann, Martin, 32
Grabowski, Stanislaus J., 28
Granderath, Theodor, 39
Granfield, Patrick, 7, 11, 92, 97, 98, 105, 109, 121, 133, 134, 161
Gratsch, Edward J., 19
Greá, D. Adrien, 17
Greeley, Andrew M., 97, 103, 137
Green, James P., 130
Green, T. J., 131
Greinacher, Norbert, 79, 85, 94, 100, 158, 166
Gremillion, Joseph, 14, 138, 163
Grenn, James P., 130
Grillmeier, Aloys, 44, 127
Grisez, Germain, 119
Grollenberg, Lucas, 144
Grootaers, Jan, 47, 114, 116, 130, 154
Gros, Jeffrey, 71, 75
Gryson, Roger, 158
Guéret, Michel, 38, 41
Guillemette, François, 130
Guillet, Jacques, 21, 122
Guitton, Jean, 22
Gumbleton, T. J., 115

Gunton, Colin E., 56
Gustafson, James M., 103
Gutiérrez, Gustavo, 41, 166

Haase, Wolfgang, 56
Hagen, Kenneth, 12
Hahn, Ferdinand, 85
Haight, Roger D., 81, 86, 166
Hale, J. Russell, 85
Hall, Barbara, 12
Halton, Thomas, 25
Hamer, Jerome, 92, 150
Harakas, Stanley S., 52
Hardon, John, 36
Hardt, Michael, 109
Hardy, Daniel W., 56
Häring, Bernard, 44, 88
Häring, H., 61
Harkness, Georgia Elma, 158
Harouel, J.-L., 98
Harrington, Daniel J., 22
Harris, Maria, 151
Hasenhüttl, Gotthold, 140
Hasler, August B., 39
Hastings, Adrian, 43, 67, 85,
    114, 144
Haughey, John C., 163, 179
Hausberger, Karl, 13
Hayes, Diana L., 173
Hearne, B., 84
Hebblethwaite, Peter, 47
Heft, James, 30
Hegy, Pierre, 47
Hein, Lorenz, 12
Heinz, Gerhard, 56
Heller, Dagmar, 72
Hellwig, M. K., 162
Hemrick, Eugene F., 126

Hendrix, Scott H., 34
Hengel, Martin, 163
Hennelly, Alfred T., 166, 167
Hennesey, James, 39, 150
Hennessy, Paul K., 144
Hertling, Ludwig, 26, 92
Hesse, E., 64
Hickey, J. A., 115
Hill, Edmund, 145
Hillman, Eugene, 85, 173
Hills, Julian V., 12
Himes, Michael J., 37
Hinson, E. Glenn, 56
Hocedez, Edgar, 37
Hocking, William E., 85
Hodemaker, L. A., 87
Hodgson, Peter C., 56
Hoekendijk, Johannes C., 85
Hoffman, John S., 155
Hoffman, Ronan, 85
Hoffman, Virginia, 48
Hoffmann, Joseph, 22, 121
Hofmann, Fritz, 28
Hoge, Dean R., 145, 153
Holböck, F., 53, 67
Holden, Carol M., 139
Hollenbach, D., 163
Hollenweger, Walter J., 141
Holmberg, Bengt, 22
Holmes, J. Derek, 109
Holstein, Henri, 43
Holtzmann, Jerome J., 52
Holze, Heinrich, 92
Hoping, Helmut, 11
Horst, Fidelis van der, 39
Horst, Ulrich, 124
Houtart, François, 103
Houtepen, A., 78, 144

Hovda, R. W., 154
Howell, Patrick J., 114
Hryniewicz, Waclaw, 127
Hughes, M., 79
Huizing, Peter, 98, 105, 115, 127, 150, 161
Hultgren, Arland J., 12
Hultkrantz, Ake, 175
Hume, G. B.,115
Hunt, Robert E., 105
Huss, John, 30
Huyghe, Gérard, 150

Ibán, Ivan C., 129
Iersel, Bas van, 145
Illich, Ivan, 85
Imhof, Paul, 89
Isasi-Díaz, Ada María, 172
Izbicki, Thomas M., 30

Jaki, Stanislaus, 48
Jalland, Trevor Gervase, 109
James of Viterbo. *See* Capocci, Giacomo
Jay, Eric G., 19
Jean (Quidort) de Paris, 18
Jedin, Hubert, 43
Jegen, F., 86
Jenkins, Daniel, 56
Jenkinson, William, 85
Jiménez-Urresti, Teodoro I., 98, 122, 141
John, Eric, 110
John of Torquemada. *See* Turrecremata, Johannes de
John Paul II, 14, 76, 86, 120, 130, 145, 150, 154, 163, 177

Johnson, E. A., 112
Johnson, Luke K., 22
Jones, J., 141
Jossua, Jean-Pierre, 5, 41, 77, 88
Journet, Charles, 61
Jungmann, Josef A., 11

Kaiser, Robert B., 45
Kaitholil, George, 48
Kanyora, Musimbi A., 173
Karrer, Otto, 22
Käsemann, Ernst, 22
Kaslyn, Robert J., 92
Kasper, Walter, 48, 89, 92, 120
Kaufmann, Franz-Xaver, 98
Kee, Howard Clark, 103
Kehl, Medard, 61, 98
Kelber, Werner H., 22
Keller, Max, 64
Kelly, J. N. D., 110
Kereszty, Roch, 108
Kerkhofs, J., 144
Kern, Walter, 61, 82, 120
Khomiakov, Alexis S., 53
Kienzler, K., 92
Kilian, Sabbas, 61, 134, 138
Kinast, Robert L., 154
King, Geoffrey, 161
King, John J., 82
Kinnamon, Michael, 76
Kirch, Konrad, 39
Kirvan, John J., 124
Klausnitzer, Wolfgang, 110, 124
Kleutgen, Joseph, 15
Kline, Francis, 150
Klinger, Elmar, 12, 43, 89

Kloppenburg, Bonaventure, 43, 167

Klostermann, Ferdinand, 44, 92, 154

Knox, John, 22

Kobler, John F., 44

Kolbenschlag, Madonna, 150, 158

Kolmer, Elizabeth, 150

Komonchak, Joseph A., 41, 42, 48, 103, 120, 131, 133, 134, 146

Kress, Robert, 7, 92

Krieg, Robert A., 17

Kroeger, James H., 86

Küng, Hans, 30, 31, 48, 61, 67, 69, 73, 98, 100, 101, 105, 106, 110, 124, 125, 127, 141

Ladner, Gerhart B., 26

Laflaive, Anne, 158

Lafont, Ghislain, 101

Lamb, Matthew, 12

Lambert, Bernard, 76

Lamirande, Émilien, 28

Lang, Joseph R., 86

Langan, J. P., 163

Lanne, Emmanuel, 53, 78, 133

Las Casas, Bartolomé de, 175

Laszlo, Stephen, 69

Latourelle, René, 42, 69, 88, 89

Laurentin, René, 130, 131, 167, 177

Lauret, B., 22, 133

LaVelle, Michael, 172

LaVerdiere, Eugene A., 81, 86, 118

Lawler, J. G., 154

Lawler, Michael G., 93, 145, 148

Lawlor, Francis X., 7

Leckey, Dolores R., 154

Lecler, Joseph, 30

Leclercq, Jean, 18, 30

Lécuyer, Joseph, 115, 145

Lee, Bernard J., 48, 95

Lee, Jung Young, 174

Leeming, Bernard, 76

Légaut, Marcel, 48

Legrand, Hervé-M., 117, 131, 133

Le Guillou, Marie-Joseph, 7, 61, 76

Lehmann, Karl, 79, 110

Lehmann, W., 64

Leith, John H., 56

Lemaire, André, 145

Lennan, Richard, 48, 154

Leo XIII, 14

Lerch, Joseph R., 7

Lettmann, Reinhard, 131

Leys, Ad, 106

Lienhard, Joseph T., 26, 145

Lienhard, Marc, 34

Lim, Byeung-Hun, 174

Limouris, Gennadios, 53

Linan, John E., 172

Lindbeck, George A., 43, 44, 125

Lindberg, Carter, 34

Linehan, Peter, 29

Lipscomb, Oscar H., 100

Littell, F. H., 65

Lohfink, Gerhard, 22
Löhrer, Magnus, 23, 67
Lohse, Eduard, 22
Lombardi, Riccardo, 82
López-Illana, Francesco, 133
Lorcin, Marie-Thérèse, 12
Lossky, Nicholas, 72
Lozano, John M., 150
Lubac, Henri de, 44, 45, 61,
    62, 67, 89, 134, 177
Lutz-Bachmann, Matthias, 12
Luykx, Archimandrite Boni-
    face, 53
Luzbetak, Louis, 86
Lynch, J. E., 118
Lytle, Guy F., 30

Maccarrone, Michele, 110
MacDonald, Margaret Y., 23
MacDonald, Timothy I., 48
MacEoin, Gary, 110, 131
MacGregor, Geddes, 56
Mackie, Robert, 12
Macquarrie, John, 145
Maduro, Otto, 11
Magaña, Alvaro Quiroz, 167
Magistretti, Franca, 42
Maguire, William E., 18
Mahan, Brian, 167
Malherbe, Abraham, 23
Malkes, Catharina, 177
Malmberg, Felix, 64
Mandouze, André, 113
Manns, Peter, 34
Mansi, J. D., 15, 16
Manson, T. W., 79
Marciniak, E., 152
Margull, Hans, 127

Marins, José, 95
Mariotti, Mario, 132
Maritain, Jacques, 62
Markus, Robert, 110
Marquart, Kurt E., 57
Martelet, Gustave, 150
Martimort, Aimé-Georges, 37,
    148
Martin, David A., 103, 141
Martin, Francis, 158
Martin, Ralph P., 23, 86
Martin, Victor, 37
Martínez, Dolorita, 172
Marty, Martin E., 163
Matovina, Timothy M., 171
May, E., 120
May, Georg, 110
May, William W., 120
Mazzoni, Giampietro, 115
McBrien, Richard P., 48, 62,
    101, 110, 115, 145, 180
McCann, Dennis, 167
McCarthy, Timothy G., 48
McCaslin, Patrick, 148
McCord, Peter J., 110
McCormick, Richard A., 118,
    119, 120
McCue, James F., 35
McDonagh, Enda, 84, 86, 150
McDonald, Kevin, 178
McDonnell, Kilian, 34, 76, 141
McGavran, Donald A., 85
McGovern, Arthur F., 168
McGovern, James O., 76
McKelvey, R. J., 23
McKenzie, John L., 120
McManus, Eamon, 75
McManus, Frederick, 108, 131

McNamara, Jo Ann Kay, 151
McNamara, Kevin, 44, 62
McPartlan, Paul, 89
McShane, Philip A., 26
McSorley, Harry, 34
Meeks, Wayne A., 23
Meier, John P., 20
Melloni, Alberto, 13
Melton, J. Gordon, 73
Ménard, Étienne, 32, 49
Menges, Walter, 79
Menozzi, Daniele, 13
Meo, Salvatore M., 177
Mercado, Edwin E., 174
Mersch, Émile, 26, 64
Mertens, H. E., 127
Messori, Vittorio, 50
Metz, Johann B., 101, 162, 163
Meyendorff, John, 53, 110, 111
Meyer, Harding, 34, 35, 71
Michonneau, Georges, 138
Miguez Bonino, José, 168
Miller, Donald E., 146
Miller, Edward J., 37
Miller, J. Michael, 111
Miller, John H., 44
Mills, C. W., 104
Milner, Benjamin C., 35
Minear, Paul S., 23, 57
Minnerath, Roland, 49, 115
Minnich, Nelson H., 35
Minus, Paul, 76
Mitchell, Nathan, 145
Moberg, David O., 103
Moeller, C., 44
Mohler, James A., 145
Möhler, Johann Adam, 18

Moingt, J., 121
Molinari, Paolo, 69
Mollat, G., 35
Moloney, Francis, 151
Moltmann, Jürgen, 57, 106
Moltmann-Wendel, Elizabeth, 158
Monahan, Arthur P., 18
Mondin, G. Battista, 28, 49, 62
Montague, George T., 141
Montcheuil, Yves de, 62
Moore, Peter, 115
Moran, Gabriel, 151
Morgante, Marcello, 134
Morrisey, Francis G., 120
Mörsdorf, Klaus, 115
Motte, Mary, 86
Mudge, Lewis S., 57, 77
Mühlen, Heribert, 62, 77, 141
Mullen, Peter, 141
Müller, Alois, 85, 100, 106, 177
Müller, Hubert, 128, 131, 161
Mund, Hans-Joachim, 111
Mura, Ernest, 64
Murphy, Charles M., 115
Murphy, Francis X., 110, 131
Murphy, Roland, 145
Murphy, T. Austin, 76, 108, 119, 126
Murphy-O'Connor, Jerome, 89
Murray, Robert, 26
Musser, Donald W., 5
Mussner, Franz, 111
Musto, Ronald G., 168

Nadeau, Marie Thérèse, 49

Nassif, Bradley, 13, 91
Naud, André, 120
Navarrette, Urban, 98
Navarro Lisbona, Antonio, 89
Neal, Marie Augusta, 151
Nealen, Mary Kaye, 168
Nédoncelle, Maurice, 37
Neill, Stephen Charles, 73
Neiman, David, 13
Nelson, J. Robert, 57, 110
Neuhaus, Richard John, 146, 162
Neuner, Peter, 13, 67
Neunheuser, Burkhard, 134
Newbigin, Lesslie, 57
Newman, John Henry, 39, 161
Newsome, Robert R., 138
Nichols, Aidan, 6, 53, 146
Nichols, Terence L., 106
Nickoloff, James B., 172
Niebuhr, H. Richard, 103, 146, 180
Nilson, Jon, 77, 121
Nissiotis, Nikos A., 53
Noble, Thomas F. X., 111
Nolte, J., 61
Nørgaard-Højen, Peder, 11
Norgren, William, 77
Norris, Frank B., 64
Novak, Michael, 45, 152, 168
Nowell, Robert, 148
Nygren, Anders, 57

Oakley, Francis, 31
O'Brien, David J., 15, 163
O'Brien, John, 168
O'Callaghan, Paul, 70
Ochoa, Xaverius, 41

O'Collins, Gerald, 88
O'Connor, James T., 124
O'Dea, Thomas F., 49, 103
O'Donnell, Christopher, 7
O'Donovan, Leo J., 13, 49, 120
Oduyoye, Mercy Amba, 173
O'Gara, James, 138, 154
O'Gara, Margaret, 77, 125
Ogden, Schubert M., 168
O'Grady, Colm, 57
O'Grady, John F., 62, 146
O'Halloran, James, 95, 96
Ohlig, Karl-Heinz, 111
Oldham, Joseph, 58
O'Leary, Paul P., 53
Olin, John C., 35
Oliver, Robert W., 155
O'Malley, John W., 44, 101
O'Meara, Thomas F., 37, 146
O'Murchu, Diarmuid, 151
Onclin, W., 117
O'Neill, Colman E., 32, 80
Orna, Mary Virginia, 106
O'Rourke, John J., 134
Orsy, Ladislas M., 121, 151
Osawa, Takeo, 161
Osborne, Kenan B., 146, 155
Osiek, Carolyn, 23, 146, 159
O'Sullivan, Helene, 85

Padberg, J. W., 150
Page, John R., 125
Pagé, Roch, 128, 134
Pairault, C., 121
Pallath, Paul, 49
Palmer, William, 37
Panikulam, George, 93

Pannenberg, Wolfhart, 57, 58, 66, 180
Pannizzolo, S., 10
Papin, J., 179
Parent, Rémi, 155
Parish, Helen, 175
Parrella, F., 134
Pascoe, Louis B., 31
Passaglia, Carlo, 18
Patelos, Constantine, 54
Pathil, Kuncheria, 174
Paul VI, 15, 86
Peck, George, 155
Pelchat, Marc, 49
Pelikan, Jaroslav, 8
Pellicia, Guerrino, 149
Pellitero, Ramiro, 155
Pelton, Robert S., 65
Pennington, Kenneth, 111
Peri, Vittorio, 128
Perri, William D., 146
Perrin, Norman, 180
Perrin-Jassy, Marie France, 96
Pesch, R., 110
Peter, Carl J., 101
Petri, Heinrich, 176
Phan, Peter C., 13, 170
Philips, Gérard, 44, 155
Pierce, Gregory, 153
Pieris, Aloysius, 174
Pineda, Ana Maria, 172
Pinto de Oliveira, Carlos-Josephat, 13
Piolanti, Antonio, 177
Piubert, Roger, 124
Pius XII, 15
Plater, Ormonde, 148
Plumpe, Joseph C., 26

Poling, James N., 146
Poma, A., 120
Pomazansky, Michael, 54
Portillo, Alvaro Del, 155
Pottmeyer, Hermann Josef, 41, 61, 92, 98, 110, 111, 125, 131
Poulat, E., 98
Powell, John, 62
Power, David N., 144, 146, 152, 155
Power, John, 86
Preston, Geoffrey, 49
Preus, Herman A., 35
Price, Bernard, 131
Price, Joseph L., 5
Provost, James H., 86, 92, 115, 121, 146
Prusak, B., 134
Przewozny, Bernard, 89

Quade, Quentin L., 168
Quebedeaux, Richard, 141
Quinn, Bernard, 138
Quinn, John R., 111, 150

Rademacher, William J., 138, 155
Rahner, Hugo, 9, 26, 138, 177
Rahner, Karl, 7, 44, 45, 49, 65, 70, 75, 80, 82, 86, 87, 89, 106, 116, 121, 125, 141, 150, 155, 162, 164
Raines, John, 11
Raiser, Konrad, 77
Ramsey, Paul, 164
Rankin, David, 26
Ratzinger, Joseph, 28, 44, 49,

50, 65, 77, 79, 93, 116, 164, 177
Rauch, Albert, 89
Rausch, Thomas P., 96, 112
Reding, Marcel, 13, 30
Reese, Thomas J., 98, 99, 131
Refoulé, F., 22, 133
Rémy, Jean, 103
Repgen, K., 43
Rettenbach, N. B., 11
Reumann, John, 93, 107
Richard, Lucien, 44
Richesin, L. Dale, 167
Richey, Russell E., 104
Riedl, Alfons, 121
Rigal, Jean, 93, 101
Riggs, Ann, 75
Rikhof, Herwi, 50, 116
Rivera, A., 176
Roberson, Ronald G., 73
Robert, D. J., 11
Roberts, J. Deotis, 173
Robinson, John A. T., 65
Rocca, Giancarlo, 149
Rodriguez, Pedro, 134
Roozen, David A., 87
Röper, Anita, 82
Rosado, Caleb, 172
Rosales, Gaudencio B., 174
Rouse, Ruth, 73
Rousseau, Olivier, 125
Routhier, Gilles, 44
Roy, Paul S., 138
Ruether, Rosemary Radford, 50, 100, 159, 168, 180
Ruggieri, Giuseppe, 13, 77
Runyon, Theodore, 58
Rusch, William G., 71, 77

Russell, Letty M., 159
Ryan, A. S., 39
Ryan, John J., 31
Ryle, Edward, 164
Rynne, Xavier, 45

Sabra, George, 33
Saier, Oskar, 93
Salaverri, Ioachim, 62
Sanchez, R. F., 115
Sanks, T. Howland, 13, 50, 62, 121
Santa Ana, Julio de, 164
Sartori, L., 50
Sartory, T., 53, 67
Satgé, John de, 111
Sauras, Emilio, 7, 80
Scannone, Juan Carlos, 11
Scazzoso, Piero, 26
Schaff, David S., 30
Schall, James V., 168
Scharper, Philip, 166
Schatkin, Margaret, 13
Schatz, Klaus, 39, 111, 125
Schauf, Heribert, 116
Schaull, R., 166
Scheele, H.-W., 34
Scherer, James A., 87
Schillebeeckx, Edward, 50, 64, 80, 89, 116, 122, 133, 144, 146, 147, 155, 164, 177
Schimmelpfenning, Bernhard, 112
Schindler, David L., 93
Schineller, J. P. 49, 81
Schineller, Peter, 170
Schlette, Heinz Robert, 82

Schlier, Heinrich, 23
Schlink, Edmund, 44, 58, 77
Schmaus, Michael, 62
Schmemann, Alexander, 54
Schmidt, Karl Ludwig, 23, 180
Schnackenburg, Rudolf, 23,
    65, 66, 180
Schner, George P., 45, 147
Schockenhoff, Eberhard, 13
Schoenherr, Richard A., 147
Schönborn, Christoph, 180
Schönmetzer, Adolfus, 45,
    114, 122
Schoonenberg, P., 122
Schrader, Clemens, 18
Schreiter, Robert J., 171, 172
Schürmann, Heinz, 141
Schütte, Heinz, 35
Schwaiger, Georg, 13, 128
Schwartz, Reinhold, 99
Schweizer, Eduard, 24, 65
Searle, Mark, 138
Sears, R. T., 81
Seckler, Max, 11, 33, 61, 120,
    121
Segovia, Fernando F., 24
Segundo, Juan Luis, 168, 169
Selling, Joseph A., 130
Semmelroth, Otto, 44, 89,
    164, 177
Senior, Donald, 24, 87
Sesboüé, Bernard, 50, 156,
    161
Seumois, André, 87
Shanahan, Thomas J., 93
Shannon, Thomas A., 15, 163
Sharkey, Michael, 61
Shaw, Russell, 156

Shea, J., 144
Sheerin, John B., 72
Sherman, Lynn C., 148
Sherrard, Philip, 112
Shook, L. K., 45
Shorter, Aylward, 87, 171
Shriver, Peggy L., 73
Shriver, S., 152
Shugrue, Timothy J., 148
Sieben, Hermann Josef, 128,
    131
Skydsgaard, Kristen E., 65,
    180
Smith, Christian, 169
Smith, John Holland, 31
Smith, Robert D., 70
Smulders, Peter, 90
Sobrino, Jon, 166, 169
Sommerfeldt, J., 36
Song, Choan-Seng, 174
Spindler, M. R., 87
Spinka, Matthew, 31
Stacpoole, Alberic, 45, 178
Stafford, J. Francis, 176
Staniloe, Dumitru, 54
Stanley, David M., 24, 116, 180
Starkloff, Carl F., 175
Steinacker, Peter, 67
Stendahl, Krister, 24
Stöhr, Johannes, 70
Stone, Bryan P., 147
Stormon, E. J., 71
Stransky, Thomas F., 72, 83
Stuhlmueller, Carroll, 24, 87
Suenens, Léon Joseph, 116,
    142
Sugirtharajah, R. S., 174

Sullivan, Francis A., 45, 63, 67, 82, 92, 121, 122, 142, 175
Sullivan, Lawrence E., 175
Sullivan, Teresa, 137
Swan, Darlis J., 75
Sweazey, George E., 87
Sweetser, Thomas, 139
Swidler, Arlene, 116, 159
Swidler, Leonard, 106, 116, 122, 124, 159
Swiezawski, Stefan, 31
Sykes, Stephen, 58

Tarago, Yolanda, 171
Tavard, George H., 37, 58, 63, 147, 159, 178
Tekippe, Terry J., 125
Tessarolo, Andrea, 134
Thaler, Anton, 90
Theisen, Jerome P., 82
Theissen, Gerd, 24
Théobald, Ch., 50
Thils, Gustave, 36, 37, 40, 67, 78, 112, 116, 124, 125, 156, 161
Thompson, Michael B., 10
Thompson, William G., 81
Thompson, William M., 161
Thurian, Max, 78
Thwaites, Reuben Gold, 175
Tierney, Brian, 29, 31, 108, 124, 125
Tillard, Jean-Marie R., 93, 112, 134, 151, 161
Tilley, Terrence W., 112
Tilon, P., 50
Todd, John M., 122, 127
Tombeur, Paul, 38, 41

Tomka, Miklos, 77
Tomko, Josef, 131
Torrance, Thomas F., 35
Torrell, Jean-Pierre, 40, 116, 124
Torres, Sergio, 96, 169
Toschi, Massimo, 13
Tracy, David, 77, 101
Trevisan, T. M., 95
Troeltsch, Ernst, 104
Tromp, Sebastian, 65
Tsirpanlis, Constantine N., 54
Tuell, Jack M., 117
Turrecremata, Johannes de, 18

Ullmann, Walter, 31, 112
Urban, Hans Jörg, 107
Urtasun, J., 150
Useros Carretero, Manuel, 33
Uzukwu, Elochukwu E., 173

Vagaggini, C., 36
Vajta, H., 34
Valentini, Donato, 50, 116
Valeske, Ulrich, 6, 50
Vandenakker, John Paul, 96
Vander Gucht, Robert, 47
Vanderwilt, Jeffrey, 78
Vanni, U., 154
Vapos, Nomikos Michael, 53
Varacalli, Joseph A., 104
Vecsey, Christopher, 175
Vela, Jesús Andrés, 96
Ven, Johannes A. van der, 104
Verbraken, Patrick, 24
Verstraelen, F. J., 87
Veuillot, P., 117

Vidal, Maurice, 65
Vilela, Albano, 147
Villar, José R., 134
Vischer, Lukas, 71, 78
Visser't Hooft, Wilhelm A., 58, 74
Viviano, Benedict T., 180
Volf, Miroslav, 58
Volk, Hermann, 10
Vollebergh, J. J. A., 144
Vollert, Cyril, 178
Vooght, Paul de, 31
Vorgrimler, Herbert, 11, 25, 28, 44, 47, 68, 74, 84, 115, 126, 145, 154, 164, 180
Vries, Wilhelm de, 54, 128

Wagner, Harald, 10, 13
Wainwright, Geoffrey, 78
Walf, Knut, 98, 99, 115, 127, 161
Wallace, Ruth A., 139, 153
Walls, Andrew F., 87
Walter, Peter, 13
Ware, Timothy (Kallistos), 54
Warnach, Viktor, 24
Wasselynck, René, 147
Weakland, R. G., 115
Weber, Max, 104
Weiler, Anton, 126
Weitlauff, Manfred, 13
Welch, Claude, 58

Wenger, Antoine, 45
West, Charles, 12
Whitehead, Evelyn E., 139, 144, 147, 156
Whitehead, James D., 139, 144, 147, 156
Wicks, Jared, 26, 35, 92
Willebrands, Johannes, 93
Willems, Boniface, 80
Williams, Colin W., 58
Williamson, Peter, 86
Wilmore, Gayraud S., 173
Wilson, Bryan R., 104
Winninger, Paul, 148
Winter, Gibson, 104
Witte, Jan. L., 66, 67, 68
Wittstadt, Klaus, 12, 43, 89
Wojtyla, Karol, 45. *See also* John Paul II
Wood, Susan K., 93
Wulf, Friedrich, 44, 151

Yarnold, Edward, 78
Yoder, John Howard, 164
Young, Lawrence A., 147
Yuhaus, Cassian J., 151

Zagano, Phyllis, 112
Zbignievus, Joseph T., 135
Zehnle, Richard, 24
Zimmermann, Marie, 99, 104
Zizioulas, J. D., 54
Zizola, G. 110